STAMP-A-BIRTHDAY

STAMP-A-BIRTHDAY

*Judy Ritchie, Kate Schmidt,
and Jamie Kilmartin
Stamp designs by Judy Pelikan*

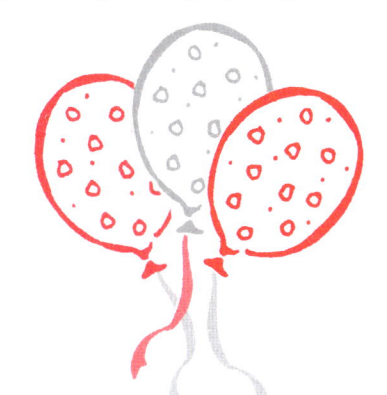

HUGH LAUTER LEVIN ASSOCIATES, INC.

Copyright © 1998 by Hugh Lauter Levin Associates, Inc.

Stamp designs © 1998 by Judy Pelikan
Line drawings by Susan Swan

All of the *Stamp-A-Birthday*™ projects have been created by Judy Ritchie,
of The Great American Stamp Store in Westport, CT

Printed in China
ISBN 0-88363-929-7

Stamp-A-Birthday™ is a trademark of All Night Media, San Rafael, CA.
and is used under license.
All Night Media, Inc., was a pioneer in the art of rubber stamping
and has been creating innovative rubber stamp products for twenty years.
You can find their quality products at gift, toy, craft, and
bookstores nationwide.

Distributed by Publishers Group West

STAMP-A-BIRTHDAY

INTRODUCTION 6

GETTING STARTED 9
The STAMP-A-BIRTHDAY™ Kit 10
Brush Markers 12
Cleaning Your Stamps 13
Supplies You Will Need 14

BASIC INKING TECHNIQUES 15
Inking with a Die Ink Pad 16
Inking with Water-Based Markers 17
Inking with Pigment Inks 19
Inking with Rainbow Ink Pads 20
Inking with Other Inks 21
Using Bleach for Special Effects 21

PLANNING YOUR PROJECT 23
The Basics 24
Choosing and Knowing Your Papers 24
Planning Your Layout 27
Repeated Images 30
Masks 33
Frames and Borders 35
The Stamp Positioner 37

CREATING BACKGROUNDS 39
Sponging 40
Spattering 41
Using a Brayer 41
Roller Stamps 44

ADDING COLOR AND SPARKLE 45
Colored Pencils and Markers 46
Watercolor 46
Chalks 48
Glitter 49

EMBOSSING 51
Embossing with Ink 52
The Embossing Process 53
Special Embossing Techniques 55
Multiple Powders on One Image 55
Embossing a Frame or Border 56
Double Embossing 57

MOVING ON 59
3-D Effects and Shadows 60
The Illusion of Motion 62
Pop-Ups and Pop-Outs 62
Reversing an Image 65
Fabric Stamping 66
Stamping on Wood and Other Surfaces .. 70
Mounting Stamps 71
Making a Stamp 72
Carving a Stamp 72
Using the Computer 73
Patterns 74
Templates 74
Numerals 74

STAMP-A-BIRTHDAY™ SPECIAL PROJECTS 79
How to Make the Projects 89

Introduction

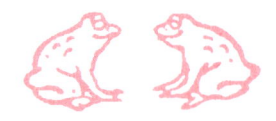

Everyone likes to be remembered at birthday time. Grownups might not have as many parties as they did when they were children, but they still look forward to receiving birthday cards. Even more special is receiving a card that someone has made just for you. It is a wonderful feeling to know that someone has taken the trouble to make you your own card, and also to know that no one else has been sent that very same card.

For instance, can you imagine how pleased a grandparent would be to receive a birthday card designed and stamped by his or her grandchild?

Lucky for all of us, we do not have to be artists to design beautiful greeting cards, stationery, and packaging—rubber stamping makes it easy! And it's fun too! All you need to get started are several rubber stamps, an ink pad and/or a set of brush-marker pens, different kinds of paper, and a few simple accessories.

Rubber stamping is a perfect activity for today's busy lifestyles, and it can be enjoyed by people of all ages, from children in kindergarten to groups of senior citizens in retirement homes or alone in the quiet of their own homes. Of course, rubber-stamping activity groups can be started anywhere and with all types and ages of participants—just like reading groups or other intimate activity groups.

If you have been blessed with creative ability you can challenge yourself to create professional-looking greeting cards and packages that will dazzle your friends and relatives, and may even encourage them to create their own greeting cards and accessories. If you own a small business you may even want to incorporate some of your stamping skills into promotional pieces that give a new look to your business mailings.

$\mathcal{T}$he *Stamp-A-Birthday*™ kit contains: 25 art rubber stamps designed just for this kit to create birthday greetings for everyone on your list; red, blue, and black brush markers; red, blue, purple, yellow, brown, and green colored pencils; and a specially designed template of numbers. Also included in the kit are 6 handmade-paper cards; 6 blank white greeting cards with envelopes to get you started; brass ornaments/charms with gold ties; and a pair of decorative-edged scissors.

$\mathcal{Y}$our stamping kit includes all you need to create fancy borders, personalized gift tags, decorated envelopes, wrapping paper, or even a gift of handstamped stationery, tea towels, or a special garden sign. You will probably come up with many new ideas of your own. With a little imagination there is no limit to what you can accomplish with the *Stamp-A-Birthday*™ kit.

$\mathcal{J}$ust spend a few minutes learning the basics of rubber stamping, which are clearly outlined in the introductory sections of this book. Once you have become acquainted with the *Stamp-A-Birthday*™ instructions and helpful pictorial guides you will be able to create designs that will surely impress your family and friends, and give you creative satisfaction.

$\mathcal{N}$aturally, every person using the *Stamp-A-Birthday*™ kit will have his or her own way of approaching a stamping project. This guide offers suggestions on how to stamp and what types of items you may be able to create, but you are not bound to do it our way. In fact, we encourage you to let your own ideas and personality shine through in everything you do. Most of all, we hope you will be completely comfortable with the approach you take. If your designs please you, they are sure to please the recipients of your birthday cards.

$\mathcal{Y}$ou will find that rubber stamps are wonderfully versatile tools. By combining them in different ways you can achieve many interesting effects. All of the stamps in the *Stamp-A-Birthday*™ kit have been specially designed, not only to work together, but also to fit into the rest of your stamp collection. Look at the section of this guide called *Stamp-A-Birthday*™ Special Projects starting on page 79 to see how we have combined some of the stamps to create some magical designs.

*I*f you are already familiar with the basics of rubber stamping you may want to concentrate on the Special Projects section.

*U*sing the stamps in different ways and in different combinations not only provides you with more images to work with, but also helps you to stretch your imagination and tap your creativity. Try to look at your overall stamp collection with a fresh eye by isolating the many elements and then seeing how you can use parts of the stamps separately as well as combining them with other stamps. For example, notice how we have used the streamer stamp to create flowers on sample project number 28.

*T*he *Stamp-A-Birthday*™ kit gives you everything you need to complete hundreds of different projects. In the already mentioned Special Projects section we show you how to make 50 projects, but there is no reason why you cannot come up with many more. Don't be limited by the basic elements in the kit; explore every possibility.

*F*eel free to use your rubber stamps in combination with, for instance, other inks, markers, paper, glue, or glitter. Don't overlook all the tools around you—bits of ribbon, string, paper, buttons, postage stamps, or dried flowers—anything at all that can help you produce interesting stamping projects. Take a nature walk with a child to collect items to include in your stamping projects—leaves, acorns, bark, shells, sand, etc.

*M*any stampers prefer working with stamps that are mounted on wooden blocks. If you would like to wood-mount the stamps in this kit see page 71.

*W*e hope this book inspires you to use your stamps creatively to express yourself. You will surprise and delight your family and friends with your clever, original cards and presents, uniquely hand-stamped by you.

*B*e creative and have fun!

Getting Started

THE *STAMP-A-BIRTHDAY*™ KIT

The first step in using the *Stamp-A-Birthday*™ kit is to separate the block of stamps by breaking them apart at the perforations. We like to label the back of each stamp for easy identification when working with them. Place the appropriate self-adhesive stamp label (also included in the kit) on each stamp, as explained in the following paragraph.

To prepare the labels, peel away the stamp images from the sticker paper that is placed on top of the stamps in the kit. Position and stick the cut-out label onto the top of the appropriate stamp, making sure that the sticker image is oriented in the same direction as the image on the stamp. If you would like to protect the labels, cover each with heavy transparent packing tape or clear contact paper. Be sure to trim the excess tape so that it is flush with the stamp block.

It is best to store your stamps with the rubber side down, out of direct sunlight and away from heat and dust. Excess heat and the ultraviolet rays in sunlight can harden and dry out the rubber, making the stamps unusable.

Before you actually begin to stamp,

prepare a comfortable working area for yourself. You can usually get the sharpest images and best results by working on a cushioned surface, such as a newsprint pad, a computer mouse pad, or a magazine. A newsprint pad is especially helpful because it can function both as a cushion and as scrap paper.

Tip: Always open your cards and lay them flat so you have an even surface on which to stamp. If you try to stamp with the card folded, the ink may not adhere properly at the double-folded edge of the card. When you stamp on envelopes or paper bags, slip a piece of flat, thin cardboard inside, between the two surfaces, for the best stamping results.

The kind of image on a stamp dictates how to stamp so that the whole design is printed evenly. For example, large stamps or stamps with large solid areas require more ink and pressure than finely detailed stamps. Apply pressure evenly as you stamp directly down on the paper. Hold the stamp with one hand while pressing evenly on the top of the stamp with the other. To avoid blurring the image be careful not to rock or wiggle the stamp. To avoid smudging, wait until a print is dry before stamping next to it.

Because each stamp has its own peculiarities (some stampers might even say "personality") it is important to make test prints on scrap paper before stamping on your good paper. You can then make adjust-

Hold the stamp firmly with one hand and press down on the stamp, rotating your finger evenly across the back of the stamp.

ments to accommodate the peculiarities of the stamps, the ink, or the paper. Don't settle for second-best when making final prints.

BRUSH MARKERS

The brush markers in this kit contain water-based ink, and are usable on all kinds of papers. Remember to cap your markers when they are not in use to prevent them from drying out.

Sometimes you will not want to use the entire image stamp. The markers we have provided in the *Stamp-A-Birthday*™ kit allow you to ink only a part of a stamp. You could also ink your stamps by tapping them gently on a water-based dye ink pad. Most stampers prefer actually inking the stamp directly. This also allows you to use more than one color at a time on a single stamp image.

As you can see in the Special Projects section, your stamps can be transformed into many more if you use them creatively. For example, instead of using the garden gloves in the frame you can use each one separately. You don't have to use the moon with the sun and the star every time; you can use one or the other. You could use the "bow" on top of the present itself, and it becomes fireworks; the sprig can be stamped alone, or many times to create a tree, as in project number 29. You could isolate the confetti on the "Happy Birthday" stamp and stamp it all over a card to create a festive background. There are many options that will be fun as you gain confidence designing your projects.

Don't overlook the colored pencils provided in the kit. The subtle shading and soft color you can achieve with these pencils can add another level of interest to your stamped art.

There are two kinds of paper included in the kit—the white paper cards and envelopes have a matte finish. Test how the ink from the markers works with this paper before doing any final printing. Experiment with the handmade papers included to see how they respond to the ink. You may want to cut up some of the handmade paper cards to use as layers or frames for your stamped images. You could also create a collage of stamped images, handmade papers, and "found" objects. Use the papers in this kit as a reference when purchasing additional papers for stamping. Experiment with other papers to find the one that you think is right for your specific project.

Tip: The quality and price of papers vary greatly. You do not need to spend a lot of money on high-quality papers that you may not need. It's best to see what you need before investing in any materials. Ask to see varying grades of paper when you are shopping for paper.

Cleaning a stamp using a handy cleaning plate.

CLEANING YOUR STAMPS

It is essential to clean the ink off each stamp after using or changing colors. We like to have a "cleaning plate" ready. To prepare a cleaning plate, moisten a paper towel, a sponge, or a rag with warm water, wring it out gently, and place it flat on a plate. You should also have a dry towel available to dry the stamp after it has been cleaned.

To clean the stamp, tap it gently, image-side down, several times on scrap paper to remove as much ink as possible. Then tap the stamp (image-side down) several times onto the cleaning plate and, finally, onto a clean, dry towel to remove excess moisture.

Never use harsh cleaners or alcohol-based solvents to clean your stamps. They could leave a film on the stamp or dry out the rubber. If the ink seems particularly stubborn, try scrubbing the rubber with an old toothbrush dipped in water. To remove ink from your hands, use baby wipes, or plain old soap and water.

There will probably be times when you will need to remove glitter from the stamps. Wrap a piece of double-stick tape around your fingers and gently tap the rubber to remove the glitter.

SUPPLIES YOU WILL NEED

In addition to the items included in your *Stamp-A-Birthday*™ kit, you might want to assemble the following items before you start your projects:

- dye ink pad and pigment ink pad
- rainbow ink pads
- water-based brush markers
- colored pencils or fine-tip markers
- crack-and-peel (sticker) paper
- glitter, glitter glue, and embossing papers
- embossing pens, markers, and pads
- heat gun or alternative heat source
- watercolor pencils, watercolors, and brushes
- soft chalks
- sponges and compressed cellulose sponges
- brayers (ink rollers)
- large rubber eraser or reverse-image stamp
- fabric paint or ink
- foam brushes or pads
- acrylic paints (for wood), sandpaper
- spray sealer for wood
- paper cutter, scissors, decorative scissors
- pad of paper, or some other cushioning surface
- X-Acto knife, or mat knife
- scrap paper
- plain and colored card stock
- sticky notes or thin paper for masking
- wet paper towels on a plate (a cleaning plate) or a sponge
- dry towel
- glue, and double-sided cellophane tape
- double-sided foam tape
- uncoated matte-finish gift wrap, and plain tissue paper
- ruler and positioner
- various paper punches

Basic Inking Techniques

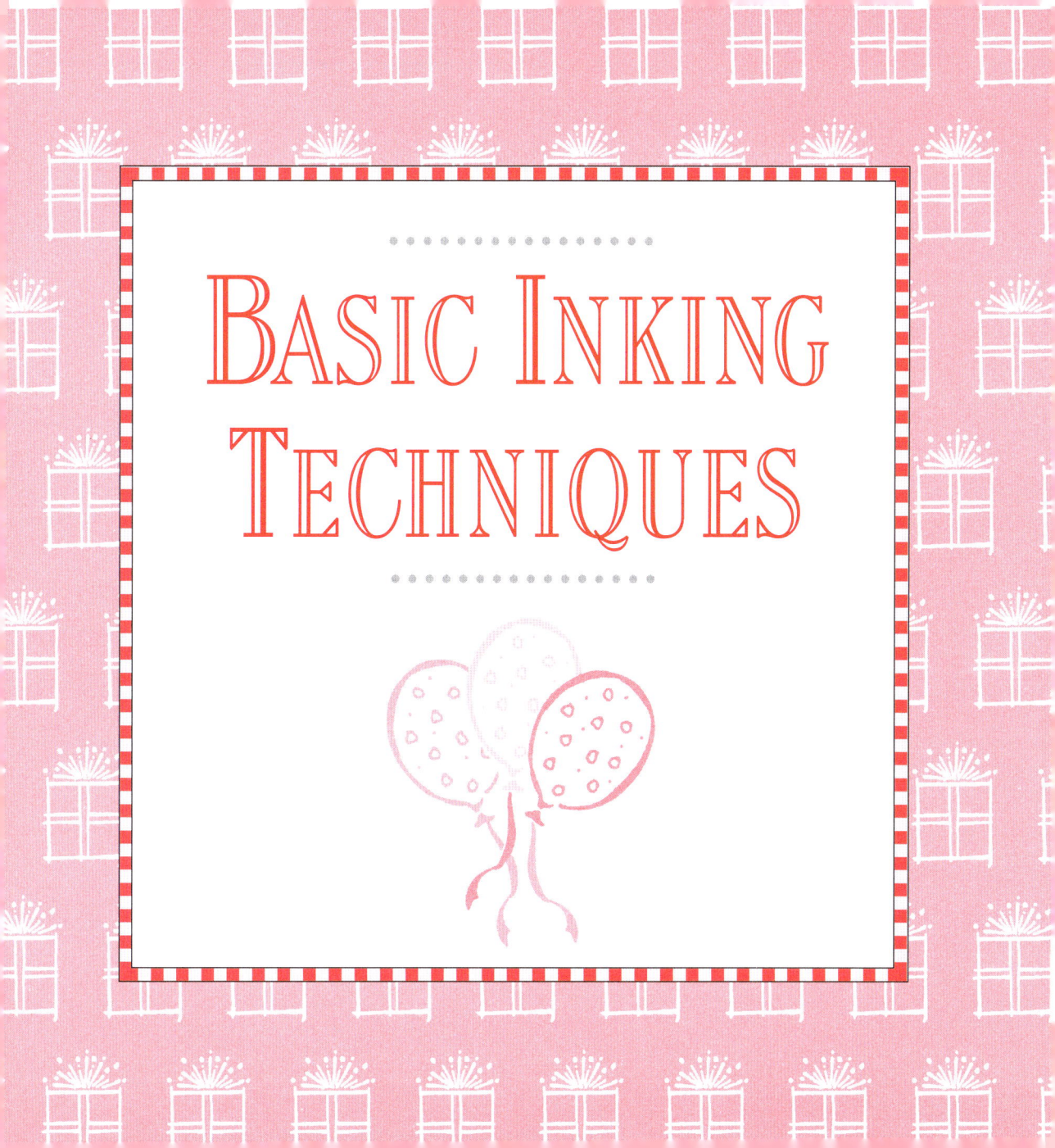

INKING YOUR STAMPS WITH A DYE INK PAD

$\mathcal{D}$ye ink, which is used in ink pads, is available in a wide range of colors, is quick-drying, and can be used on almost every kind of paper. To use an ink pad, tap the stamp gently a few times onto the ink pad and then check to make sure the whole image is covered with ink. If you press too hard, you may get ink on the rubber area surrounding the image, leaving unwanted stray marks on the paper. (If the stamp is larger than the ink pad, you may want to reverse the process, gently tapping the ink pad onto the surface of the stamp.)

$\mathcal{T}$o achieve a lighter or more subtle shade of ink, press the inked stamp on scrap paper and then, without re-inking, stamp the image on your "good" paper. This technique produces an interesting background design, which can appear under other stamped images or attractive stationery with a subtle overall pattern.

$\mathcal{A}$lways keep your stamp pad closed when it is not in use; otherwise it will dry out. And remember to store your ink pad upside down so the ink always stays on the surface, making the ink pad always ready for use.

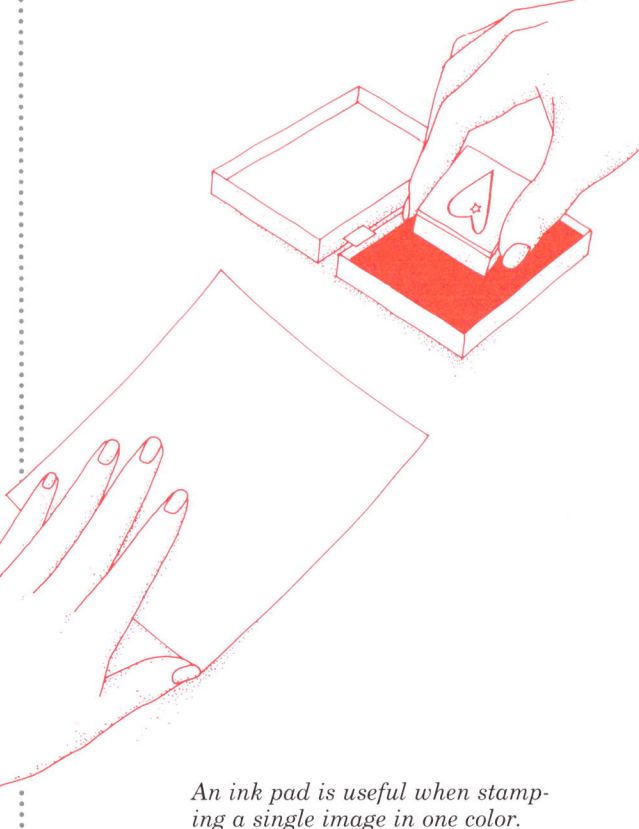

An ink pad is useful when stamping a single image in one color.

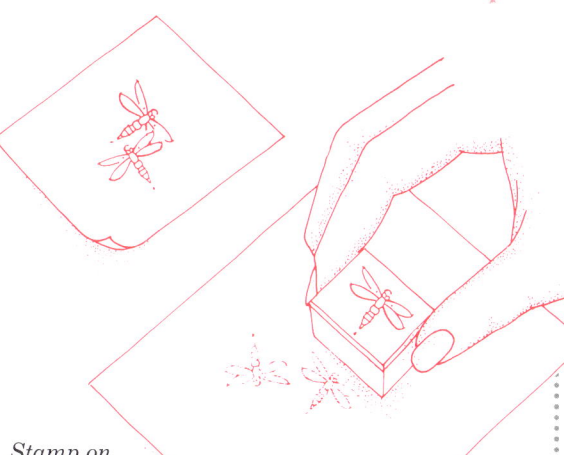

Stamp on scrap paper and then, without re-inking, stamp image again on "good" paper.

INKING WITH WATER-BASED MARKERS

$\mathscr{A}$n alternative to using an ink pad is to use water-based brush markers to ink a stamp. The brush markers in the kit contain the same kind of ink as dye ink pads, and are usable on all papers. This brush-marker alternative is our favorite way to work. (Remember to cap your markers when you are not using them to prevent them from drying out.)

$\mathscr{T}$o ink a stamp, hold the stamp in one hand with the image surface facing up, and paint directly onto the raised stamped image, using one or more colored markers. Work quickly to keep the ink from drying. If necessary, breathe gently on the stamp (with an open-mouthed "Hah") after you have inked it to add moisture to the ink just before stamping. Depending on the paper you are using, you may be able to get a second impression without re-inking the stamp by simply breathing on the stamp once again. You may also mist the stamp lightly with water from a spritz bottle. You will soon be able to judge when you need to re-ink or moisten a stamp. Practice with each stamp a few times, and it will all become second nature to you in a short time.

USING BRUSH MARKERS ALLOWS YOU TO:

❖ Ink even the largest stamps.

❖ Stamp in a wide range of colors.

❖ Stamp a multicolored image by applying different colors to different parts of the stamp.

❖ Stamp only a portion of an image.

You can color different parts of the stamp with different color inks when you use brush markers.

$\mathcal{A}$s you become more comfortable with the markers you may want to blend colors. To produce a color that is actually a blend of two colors, ink over part of the stamp that has the darker color on it (while the ink is still wet) with the lighter color pen, pulling some of the darker ink into the lighter area. When you stamp the image you will have the first two colors and a third color, which is a blend of the first two. Clean the darker ink off your brush marker by holding it on your cleaning plate until you see the true color.

$\mathcal{W}$hen inking the stamp with a brush marker, be sure to brush over the entire area you wish to stamp with the side of the marker. If you want to use more than one color, ink the stamp with the lighter color before using a darker one. This will avoid getting the darker ink on the light color.

$\mathcal{B}$ecause brush markers are very wet, you may find that you have excess ink on the paper after stamping. If you do, simply turn your finished artwork over and blot it lightly on a piece of scrap paper.

$\mathcal{T}$ip: Be sure that the markers you use on your stamps are water-based. Permanent ink could harm the rubber on the stamp.

Inking with Pigment Inks

$\mathscr{P}$igment ink, unlike dye-based ink, is opaque. This means that the color of your paper will not affect the color of the ink.

$\mathscr{P}$igment ink is available in pads of many different sizes and shapes, as well as a wide range of colors, including many metallic shades like gold, silver, bronze, and copper. Pigment ink resists fading and has a balanced pH, which minimizes acid deterioration. As a result, pigment ink is an ideal choice to use in combination with other artwork or photographs, as when creating scrapbooks or memory books.

$\mathscr{P}$igment ink is slow-drying, and requires an absorbent surface. However, if you want to use it to stamp on glossy or coated papers (which are nonabsorbent), you must emboss the ink to make it permanent. It is this slow-drying quality that makes pigment ink ideal to use when embossing on any paper. The image is stamped with pigment ink, then sprinkled with embossing powder.

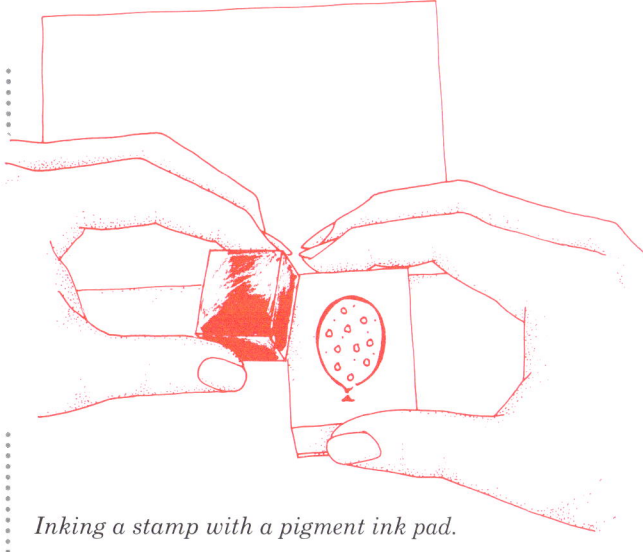

Inking a stamp with a pigment ink pad.

Heat is applied to melt the powder so that it creates a lustrous, raised image. See page 52 to learn more about embossing.

$\mathscr{T}$o ensure an even ink coverage, the best way to ink your stamp with a pigment pad is to hold the stamp in one hand with the rubber image facing up, and gently pat the entire stamp with the ink pad, which is held in the other hand. Hold the stamp at an angle in the light to see if there are any dry spots. If the stamp does not appear to be entirely wet, tap the stamp with the ink pad again. This method of inking allows you to cover even the largest stamp with a small ink pad.

Be careful not to over-ink your stamp when applying pigment ink. Because the ink is thick, over-inking will clog up the recessed areas of the stamp and make it difficult to get a clear, detailed impression. Over-inking may also cause an undesirable shadow if there is ink on the base of the stamp.

INKING WITH RAINBOW INK PADS

Using rainbow ink pads is a simple way to add variety to your stamped art because rainbow ink pads contain three or more colors or shades of the same color. They are available with both dye ink and pigment ink.

There are two methods of manufacturing dye rainbow pads. The less expensive pad is created by cutting the felt pad into strips or sections and applying a different color to each section. These pads separate the colors with plastic dividers that must be removed before use. After stamping with such a pad you may be able to see the separations on your finished artwork, especially if you are using a design with a lot of solid areas. To compensate for the separations you may want to move the stamp around slightly as you tap it onto the ink pad. This ensures an even coverage of ink over the entire surface of the stamp.

Other rainbow pads are made by hand, with the application of the ink to the felt. The colors blend well as the inks flow together. Over time, the ink on all types of dye-based rainbow pads flows together, modifying the colors. To slow this process clean your stamp before use and after each impression, and always store the pad flat. Some rainbow pads separate each color when the pad is not being used to prevent the ink from blending.

Dye rainbow pads can produce dazzling results, especially on glossy or coated paper. Try using a brayer (roller) with rainbow pads to create great backgrounds.

There are also multicolored pigment ink pads that will give results similar to those of dye-based rainbow pads.

Because of the inherent properties of pigment ink the colors will never blend together on the foam pad. Tapping your stamp several times with different areas of the pad will produce a kaleidoscopic effect. If mixing the colors on your stamp has carried one color onto the top of another color on the pad, restore your pad to its original color by simply wiping it vertically with a clean, dry paper towel.

Both pigment and dye inks are available in bottles so that you can re-ink your pads when they dry out. You can also use these bottled inks to make your own rainbow pads out of an un-inked felt or foam stamp pad.

INKING WITH OTHER INKS

Many types of paints and inks can be used to stamp images. We have used both poster and acrylic paint, and metallic pens with success. If the ink or paint is water-based, try it. But you must be sure to clean your stamp thoroughly immediately after using it with these inks.

Some office ink pads contain chemicals that could dry out and damage the rubber of your stamps. Obviously, such pads should not be used.

USING BLEACH FOR SPECIAL EFFECTS

Try creating "negative" images by using bleach instead of ink. Create a pad by soaking a piece of sponge or felt in bleach. Stamp an image on dark paper and watch as the faded images appear. The shades of bleaching will vary depending upon the color and quality of the paper you use.

Planning Your Project

THE BASICS

When planning your project, you should test the colors of your inks, pencils, and markers to see how they look and how they can work together. Be sure to test colors on the same kind of paper you'll be using for your finished project.

Use your imagination and creativity to add hand-drawn elements to your designs. If you keep them simple you need not worry about the level of your drawing ability. When you have a group of stamped flowers, for instance, try adding dots with a pen to tie the whole arrangement together. Don't think you have to be a full-blown artist right off the bat. Visit a good bookstore and browse through the books in the crafts and graphic arts sections to get some ideas. Copying is not a crime unless you plan to sell your projects, and even if you do copy, your own personality and technique will always shine through. Remember, you're supposed to be having fun!

CHOOSING AND KNOWING YOUR PAPERS

A wonderful and easy way to add new dimension to your stamping projects is to use a variety of papers for layering as well as stamping. Plain white papers, colored papers, and printed pattern papers in various textures and weights are available at rubber-stamp and scrapbook stores, as well as art supply stores and printers, and it will be to your advantage to become acquainted with the many kinds of paper. (Some examples of handmade paper are included in the kit.) Be aware that some grades of paper are much more expensive than others, so make sure you are not buying expensive paper that you don't need. A knowledgeable salesperson in a rubber-stamp store or an art supply store can be a tremendous help in selecting and understanding paper.

An uncoated white card stock is easy to use and will accept all kinds of ink, making it the perfect paper for a beginner. Before purchasing paper in bulk, try experimenting with a few sheets of different kinds. Each type of paper responds to ink in its own way.

$\mathcal{Y}$ou can achieve interesting results when you tear card stock around an image you have stamped; see project numbers 8 and 19. Hold the image area firmly with one hand, and with the other hand tear the surrounding paper away. If you tear the paper forward you see a layered edge on the image side of the paper. If you tear the paper away from you the edge will be flat. Try inking the edge with a brush marker and you will notice how the layered edge absorbs the ink and becomes darker. This can be very effective when constructing a collage. A smooth-finish paper is best if you want to stamp directly on the paper. Don't overlook stamping on colored paper for example, see project number 43.

$\mathcal{T}$o achieve the brightest colors when using dye-based inks or pens, select a glossy or coated paper. Glossy paper tends to be a little slippery, so be sure to hold the paper down with one hand as you lift your stamp with the other. Pigment inks require matte paper, which has absorbing qualities that allow the pigment ink to dry. Some papers called "matte" are in fact "matte coated," and will not work with pigment ink unless the pigment-inked image is embossed.

$\mathcal{M}$any stationery stores refer to text-weight paper as one suitable for layering, letter writing, or making envelopes. In contrast, cover or index stock is most often used for making cards, gift tags, boxes, and other sturdy items.

$\mathcal{M}$any specialty papers are available. Some examples of specialty paper are marbled, metallic, handmade; some have glitter incorporated into the surface, or have a fibrous surface. Try tearing the paper to achieve a feathered edge. Wetting the area where you want to tear the paper may make it easier to tear and give you a prettier edge. Always test on a small section first. With some papers, it is best to wet the area with a paint brush dipped in water before tearing using a ruler as a guide. Experiment with both dry and wet tearing. Rulers are available with a sharp, deckled (uneven) edge to assist tearing your paper.

$\mathcal{T}$issue paper is an inexpensive paper that is wonderful for making wrapping paper or special-effect overlays that mute a design. The transparency of tissue paper lets the design show on both sides, and tissue paper makes an interesting surface when used on top of card stock.

Try using tissue paper as a background for layering. Because tissue paper is very porous, ink tends to bleed through, so it is important to protect your work surface when stamping.

Adhesive-backed paper (often referred to as "sticker-backed paper" or "crack-and-peel") is available in matte or glossy finish, and has the same inking requirements as regular matte or glossy paper. After stamping on adhesive-backed paper, cut out the image, peel off the backing, and apply the stamped image to your artwork for a layered look. Adhesive-backed paper can also be used to create gifts such as bookplates, jar labels, or general stickers. Be advised that adhesive-backed paper is usually more expensive than regular paper.

For gift wrap use Kraft paper, poster, or uncoated shelf paper in rolls. We even use 11x17 copy paper to wrap small gifts and make gift bags, or calculator paper to adorn a package. Some paper designed for gift wrap is coated and may make stamping impossible, so be sure to test before planning your project. In our project number 3 we used glossy yellow wrapping paper to wrap the package, and then we attached a separately stamped panel to it.

Your mailbox is a great paper source. Magazines, advertisements, and junk mail are often printed on unusual papers. Some of these papers can be printed on with ink alone, but others require that the image be embossed. Some of the papers are also ideal to use as a decorative background to frame a stamped image, to create a collage, or to make or line envelopes. Printed cards and invitations often have blank areas that can be used in your new creations. These can be favorite sources for gift tags. Postage stamps, new and cancelled, make wonderful additions to collage cards. Please, recycle whenever possible.

As your stamping experience grows, your awareness of new and interesting raw materials will also develop.

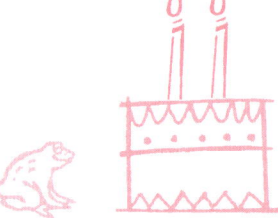

PLANNING YOUR LAYOUT

Some finished artwork looks so right you would think it just happened that way, full-blown and beautiful all on its own. But, of course, we know that designs have to be planned by someone—they don't create themselves. But by the same token, do not dismiss the notion of a design somehow looking "right," as though it could not have turned out any other way. A wonderful American painter named Richard Diebenkorn used to like to refer to the "rightness" of a finished painting, and indeed there is something "right" about a well-executed design.

Designing the layout of your project is probably the most exciting part of creating a project. Now is the time to decide what you are saying with your artwork—it's not just a pretty layout, it has a meaning and a direction that you have put there. You have inserted your own unique touch.

What do you want the recipient of your birthday card to feel? We know that bright colors are usually perceived as cheerful, soft pastels soothing, and dark colors somber or dignified. But remember, where you place an image on a page has as much effect on the viewer as the colors you choose.

The visual placement of objects on a card or package can be unpredictable and exciting, predictable and soothing, or just plain boring. By being aware of certain basic design concepts you can direct the effect your work has on its recipient. Just as the slight tilt of a head or the subtle movement of a hand can be an inviting or dismissive gesture, so too can the orientation of the elements that make up your artwork.

Let's look at a few examples that show the importance of composition. Placing a design element (the image on one of your stamps, for instance) right in the middle of your card can be effective sometimes, but not always. Although centering a design on a card may look perfect (as with wedding invitations, for example), there are times when it can look dull or unimaginative. If one of your centered designs is affecting you that way, try keeping the centered arrangement of the

This centered design fills the space nicely.

Centered elements set off-center on the page create an interesting design.

design elements, but moving them off-center on the page.

*T*ake a new look at some of your favorite classical paintings—you probably take their beauty and "rightness" for granted. The focal point of such paintings is usually somewhere off-center, creating a dynamic composition that seems to move and stay still at the same time. Also, look at our collage card project number 8.

*O*ne "trick" that we use in planning our layouts is to divide the design space into thirds horizontally and vertically (make a tic-tac-toe board), and then move the stamp images around within the boxes. The most interesting visual points are usually near the intersecting lines, so try arranging your design around one or more of those focal points, filling in the background as you feel it is needed. But please don't feel compelled to fill up all the white space on your card. Always remember that blank space is as important a design element as any of your stamps. The proper use of blank space can create a thrilling effect.

*O*n a practical note, be sure to plan your layout on scrap paper. You might find it

Dividing your space into thirds horizontally and vertically can help produce interesting layouts.

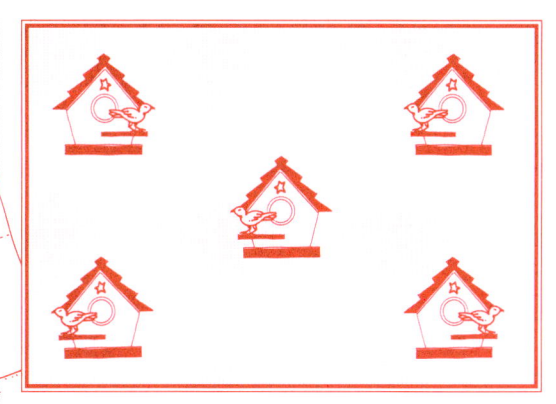

Dividing the card into a grid helps with the placement of these strong visual images.

helpful to stamp the images on paper, and then cut them out. These cut-outs are easy to move around as you try different ways to arrange your design. When you are creating a scene with stamps that are not all on the same scale or size you may want the larger elements in the foreground, with the smaller elements in the background, since that is how our eyes perceive objects. But there are no fixed rules about layout and design. Try many different versions before you choose the one you like best.

REPEATED IMAGES

One stamp can go a long way when it is used repeatedly to make patterns, borders, or clusters. Use the same color ink and stamp across the bottom, or all around the edges of a card to create a pattern or border. Try alternating colors for variety, or stamp one design and repeat it all over the card to create a background pattern or texture. If you change the angle of the stamp as you work you do not have to worry about aligning the images perfectly; see project number 21.

It is important to consider the size of the stamps you use together to form borders or repeated patterns. Stamps must work together visually if you want to create a pleasant design. For example, in project number 11 the bottom of the gift-box stamp is used to create the appropriate sized checkered border for the "Happy Birthday" stamp. The heart and the flower are the same size and complement the bold hand-drawn checkered border. If the stamps are not in the right scale, the effect could be confusing or cluttered. (Try some variations that contradict this advice, as in project number

Changing the angle of the stamp as you work means you don't have to worry about perfect alignment of the images.

The repeated image of a small cabbage rose creates a feeling of rhythm and movement.

The scale of these stamped images is well balanced; the smaller images create a nicely proportioned border to the larger centered image.

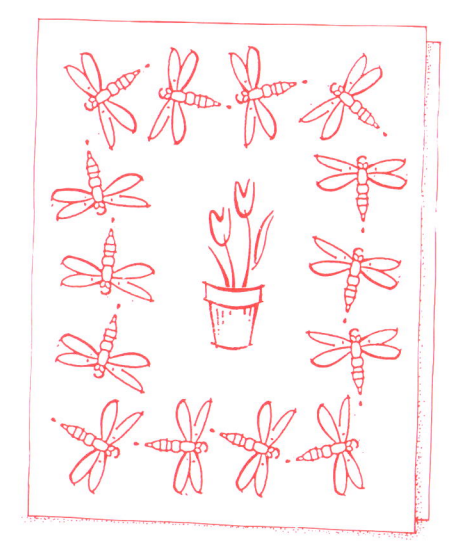

If the stamps you choose for the border are disproportionately large, the design can look haphazard.

34, where the tag is oversized to make the invitation stand out.) Sometimes exaggerating the differences in scale can create a humorous effect—remember the huge clown climbing out of a tiny car at the circus?

To ensure equal spacing when you wish to repeat the same image in a row, stamp the first image in the middle, then on the ends, and finally, in the remaining space between the ends and the middle. A stamp positioner (see page 37), ruler, or firm cardboard with a straight edge help to line up the stamps.

When you are stamping images over a large area (such as wrapping paper) one concern is that the images be spaced evenly. Use a grid to help you align and space the images. If you don't have a translucent cutting mat with a grid, prepare your own by drawing lines with a permanent marker on white paper or

Place the stamps along a straight edge ruler or cardboard to align the images on a page.

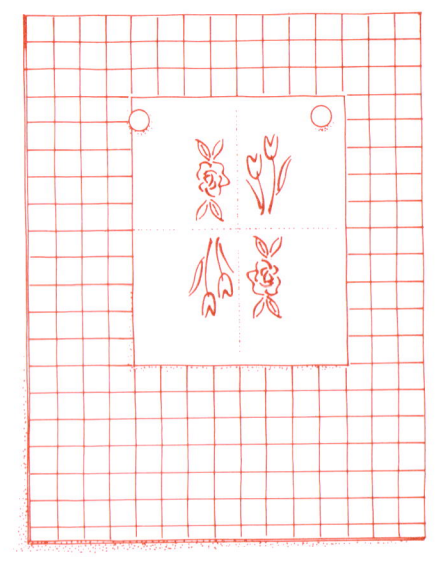

Grid paper can be used as a guide for creating straight parallel lines.

foam core. (Foam core works well because you can thumbtack your paper to it.) Lay your project over the grid and proceed with your stamping. Be sure to measure the paper and the gift to be wrapped before stamping, so you can place the stamp images most effectively, and avoid unnecessary stamping.

To create the illusion of depth when repeating images, try stamping an image in the foreground first, and then, without re-inking, stamp slightly higher on the page with the next image or two. This non-inking technique will make the images after the first one become lighter and lighter, which gives the illusion of depth.

MASKS

*C*reating a scene with rubber stamps is fun and easy to do. In fact, it is much less complicated than it looks. To create the illusion of depth in your scene, with one image appearing to be behind another, use a simple masking technique. Begin by stamping on the paper the image you want to appear closest to the viewer (in the foreground).

Stamp the flower pot on a card. Mask it and stamp the tulips in the pot.

*N*ext, stamp that same image onto a piece of thin scrap paper, or a sticky note (a trade name for these gummed pieces of paper is Post-it). The sticky part of the note should be under your impression. If you don't have a sticky note handy, use

Stamp the tulips again on thin scrap paper, allowing space for a handle.

Cut out the stamped image and the handle from the paper. This is your mask.

scrap paper, but leave a "handle" to hold, as in the drawing here. Cut out the image carefully, staying just inside the outline. This is your mask. Place the mask over the already-stamped image to protect it. Now, stamp the second image (the one you want to appear "behind" the

Place the mask over the stamped image on the card before stamping again.

Stamp new images slightly overlapping the mask. When the design is complete, remove the mask.

first one), partly overlapping the mask of the first image.

*T*o get a good, clean image you may have to increase the pressure as you stamp to compensate for the thickness of the mask and to prevent a gap between the two images. Remove the mask. You can repeat this process over and over again on the same card to accentuate the illusion of depth. By using this masking technique you will be able to place tulips in the flower pot just as if they were growing there, as in project number 47.

*O*nce you have gone to the trouble of creating a scene with masks you should certainly save the masks for future use. Maybe you plan to make a dozen cards with this design, or you might be using the stamp in a different scene. The mask can be used whenever you wish to use the stamp in combination with other stamps.

*T*ip: Store the masks you wish to keep in individual envelopes, and be sure to mark the outside of each envelope by stamping the image on it. Or you might prefer to keep the envelope in a notebook or binder with acrylic pockets or pages.

*U*sing this same masking technique, you can cover a section of paper you want to keep clean and stamp the fully inked image partially overlapping the mask.

When you want to keep the back side of a folded card free of stamped images and you want to stamp right up to the folded edge, try using a piece of paper to mask the area. Open the card and place it on your work surface with the inside facing down. Cover the back side of the card with a piece of paper (your mask) aligned at the fold, and stamp the front of the card. Some of the images can spill over onto the paper mask. Once you remove the mask you will have a straight, clean edge at the fold.

FRAMES AND BORDERS

Frames and borders are attractive design elements that can add an interesting dimension to your projects, especially when you are using small stamps. There are many ways to create a frame or border. Here is one example: Cut a shape out of paper, put it aside, and place this new template on top of your card stock. This is actually called a mortise mask or a template. Stamp the images in the "live" area—the space inside the cut-out shape, allowing some images to

Using a mortise mask of the numeral "5" to create a shaped stamped image.

overlap onto the paper of the mask itself, as shown in the illustration. When the mask is removed you will have a wonderful, clean-edged, framed design; see our project number 41.

Another way to create a frame is to pencil in a shape on a card lightly and then stamp all along the penciled line to create the shape you've drawn. After the stamp ink is dry, erase any pencil lines that show. The illustration shows a frame of clovers, but you can stamp your design in any shape you wish.

*Y*et another way to make a frame for your card is to stamp a small image the same distance away from each of the four corners of your card, and then draw lines, or dots and dashes to connect the images. As before, erase any pencil lines that show.

*A*n easy way to make a straight-line

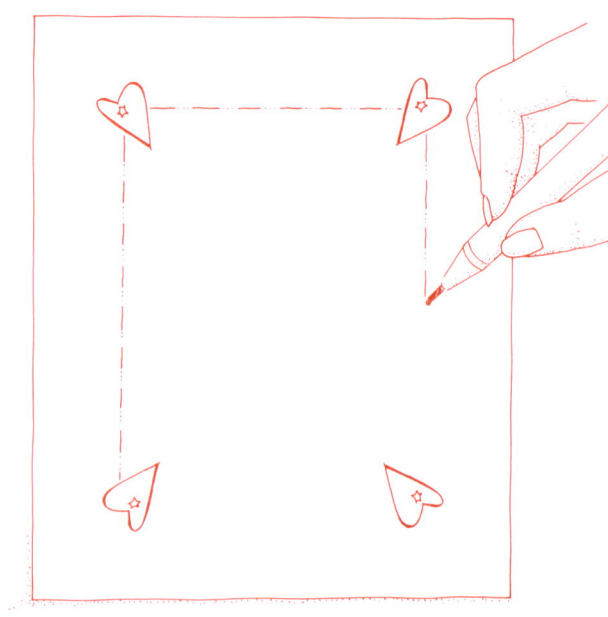

Connecting four corner images to create a frame.

A repeated pattern of four-leaf clovers creates an appealing square frame.

guide for making frames and borders is to lay your card in the middle of a large sheet of ruled notebook paper, with the card aligned on one of the ruled lines of the paper. Using another rule of the paper as a guide for your ruler, draw a straight line across the card. If you want a frame on all four sides simply rotate the card and repeat. It might be best to draw the lines lightly in pencil so that any extra marks can be erased.

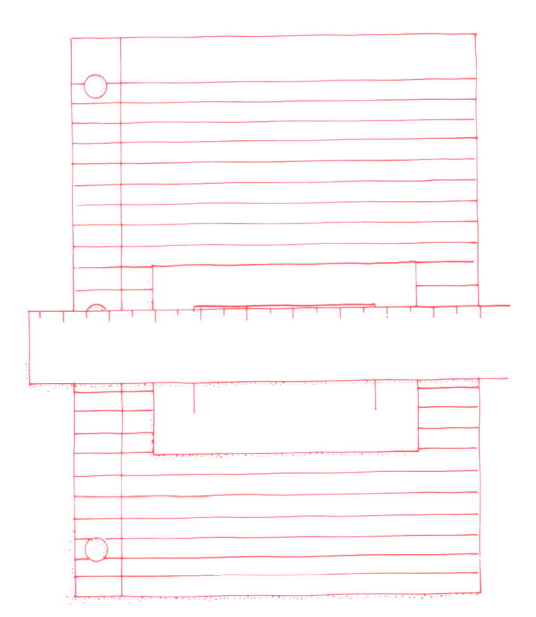

Ruled paper used as a guide for creating parallel lines.

THE STAMP POSITIONER

$\mathcal{O}$ne of our favorite tools is a stamp positioner. It helps you to place a stamped image precisely where you want it. Sometimes, no matter how careful you have been, an image is not stamped cleanly or clearly, and rather than throwing away the whole project, you can use the stamp positioner to guide the placement of a new image stamped in exactly the same spot as the defective one, right over the defective image.

$\mathcal{T}$he stamp positioner is made from two pieces of clear lucite or wood 1/2-inch thick, joined at a right angle. It is used with tracing paper or a piece of clear lucite.

$\mathcal{W}$hen using tracing paper, the first step is to color with a pen the corner edge that has been cut at a right angle. This will allow you to see that the paper is sitting snugly in the corner and has not slipped under the stamp positioner. This step is not necessary if you are using the piece of clear lucite.

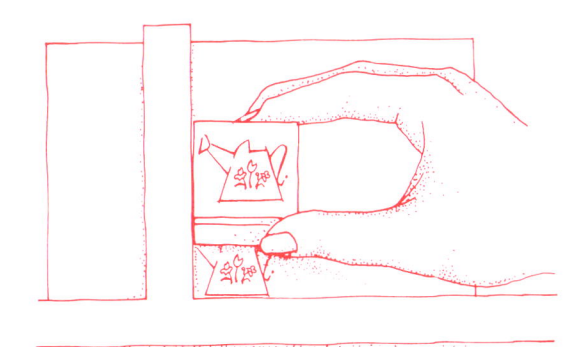

Place the stamps in the angle of the stamp positioner to align images on the page.

37

Place the piece of tracing paper or lucite snugly into the corner of the positioner. Stamp the image onto the tracing paper or lucite, being careful to slide the stamp down and along the two sides of the stamp positioner. Move the tracing-paper or lucite image around to see where you want the image stamped on your finished project. Bring the positioner to the paper or lucite, again making sure the paper or lucite fits snugly in the corner of the positioner, touching both sides. Remove the test sheet and stamp in the same spot.

You will want to retain the tracing paper to use whenever you use that particular stamp. Clean the lucite with water or stamp cleaner and a soft towel.

Positioners are also available with a base used as the stamping surface and a lucite positioner hinged to the base. This type of positioner is used most often to enhance outline images. You stamp the image first in a light color, color the image, and then re-stamp the same image in a darker color. The image can be enhanced even more by embossing the second image. (See the section on embossing on page 51.)

A stamp positioner is not essential, but it is an invaluable tool when you are creating scenes and you want precise placement of the images. It will certainly save you money by preventing stamping errors on good paper.

CREATING BACKGROUNDS

SPONGING

You can fashion a variety of backgrounds for stamped art, including an air-brushed effect, by using sponges. It is the texture of the sponge that gives the air-brushed effect. Cosmetic, porous household, and natural sponges all work well. Cosmetic sponges create a soft look, while the porous household sponge gives a mottled appearance. A background made with a natural sponge will appear lacy. There are sponges specifically designed for creating backgrounds.

Start with a dry sponge and color it with a water-based marker. If your sponge does not have round edges, gather the whole sponge up in your fingertips to prevent edges from showing.

Inking a sponge with a water-based marker.

Blot the sponge on scrap paper to remove any excess ink, and then tap it lightly all over your paper to create a soft background. For convenience, you may want to have several sponges on hand, reserving one for each color. Wash out your sponges with soapy water when you are finished with a project.

Experiment with mixing colors on your paper. For example, you can suggest a beautiful sunset by lightly layering yellows and oranges over a blue sky.

You may also apply color by tapping the sponge onto an ink pad or into any other water-based ink or paint. Metallic inks or paints give a dazzling effect to any background. Sponging over a stencil or mask of any shape is another option. Trace the cloud shape found on page 104 to cut out and form a stencil. Sponge over the edge of the stencil. For an overall cloudy sky, repeat the sponging, moving the stencil around on your paper.

Try making patterned backgrounds by sponging over netting, a paper doily, or lace. Use sponging to fill in or to give depth to stamped grass, sand, or water. A durable stencil can be made by having the cloud outline we have provided on page 104, for example, copied onto a transparency sheet. These can then be wiped off as you change colors.

*T*ry this sponging technique using all types of paper, paper towels, tissue paper, or facial tissues to provide some interesting textures. Scrunch up the sponging material in your fingers, ink it, and then tap it lightly on your paper. Each paper will produce a different effect.

SPATTERING

*S*prinkle your design with dots of color by spattering ink onto the paper with a toothbrush. Use the ink available to refill ink pads, or acrylic paint. Dilute the ink with water before dipping the toothbrush in. While holding the toothbrush over your paper, draw a knife or ice-cream stick across the brush, causing the bristles to bend. As you release, the bristles spring forward and spatter the medium onto the surface. The more paint you have on your brush, the larger the spat-

Creating a sandy background is easy using an old toothbrush to spatter the ink.

ter dots will be. It is probably a good idea to start with a relatively dry brush to produce small dots, building up the density of the dots as you see fit.

USING A BRAYER

A brayer is a small paint roller made of rubber. It was originally designed for linoleum block printing, but is another great tool to use with stamping. Use it to apply ink to the surface of your stamp or

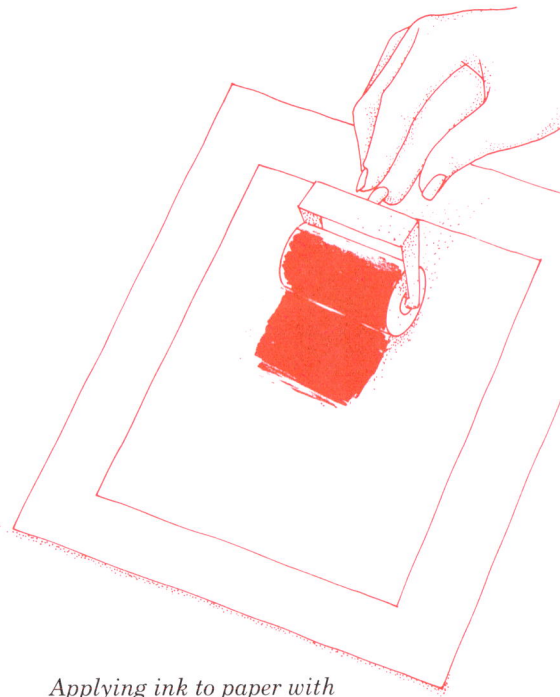

Applying ink to paper with a brayer creates a smooth background.

strokes over the ink pad or into paint poured onto a flat pan. Next, roll the smoothly inked brayer evenly over the paper or card. You can intensify the color by repeating this process. Lift the brayer between strokes, and roll in one direction only when applying ink to the paper.

Always keep scrap paper under your work so that you can roll the brayer off the edge of your artwork without staining your desk. You can create an instant sunset or colorful background for any creation with a brayer and a rainbow stamp pad. Clean your brayer just as you would clean your rubber stamps.

TRY USING THE BRAYER IN THE FOLLOWING WAYS:

directly to the paper. Brayers are available in many widths, and work well with both pigment and dye-based inks or acrylic paints. They are the best tools for applying a smooth background color to a paper surface. Using dye ink or pens produces the best results on coated paper.

To start using a brayer, cover the entire roller surface with ink, using firm

❖ Apply color on paper and then stamp an outlined or "open" image, like our gift or cake, over the color. Cut out the image and add it to your artwork for a three-dimensional or layered effect.

❖ Stamp an image using clear embossing ink, and emboss with clear embossing powder. Brayer color over the whole card. The embossed image will resist the ink,

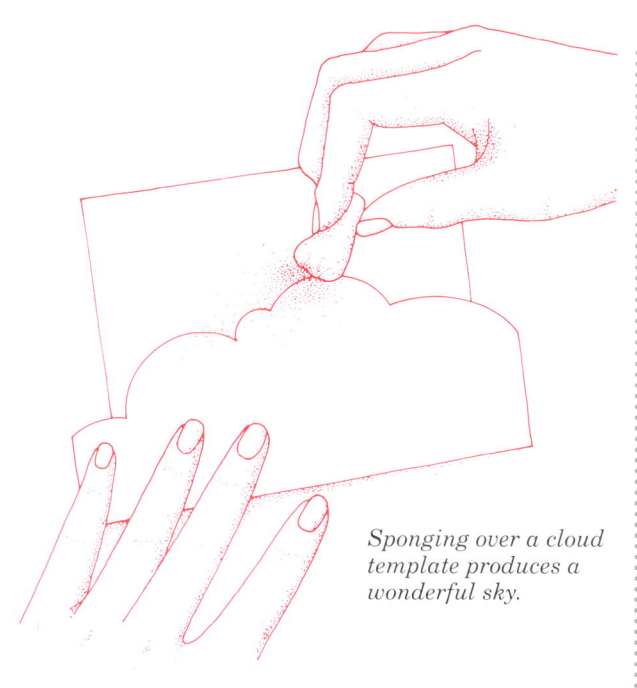

Sponging over a cloud template produces a wonderful sky.

letting the paper color show through. A quick wipe with cotton or a paper towel will remove any residue from the embossed area.

❖ You can achieve a "batik" effect by using wax or crayons with the brayer. First, draw a design on your paper with a waxy crayon. Then use your brayer to apply ink over the entire surface of the paper. The wax in the crayon will resist ink from the brayer.

❖ Create plaids by applying different inks to your paper with small brayers, then crisscrossing horizontal and vertical stripes.

❖ Use water-based markers to draw designs directly onto the brayer. Then transfer those designs to your paper with the brayer.

❖ Ink large stamps by rolling the brayer on an ink pad and then over the stamp. Stamp the image. Or make an ink "pad" by placing a few drops of refill ink onto a piece of glass. Roll the brayer through the ink to smooth it out and cover the brayer with ink. Apply the ink to the stamp. Use drops of different colors of both dye and pigment ink at the same time to produce a marbled effect.

❖ Paint a design on your card with rubber cement or a liquid masking material. When dry, brayer the color over the designs. Remove the rubber cement or masking material with a rubber-cement pickup eraser or by rubbing your fingers over it to free that area of ink.

❖ Apply Cover-Up tape, which is available in several widths, to your card to mask areas. Apply ink to the card with a brayer. When the ink is dry, rearrange the Cover-Up tape and apply a different color ink. This is an easy way to create stripes, plaids, or a crazy quilt of many colors.

ROLLER STAMPS

Specially designed roller stamps can be used in many of the same ways as a brayer. Images are repeated around the roller, forming a continuous design. Some roller stamps are even self-inking, which is ideal when you need to cover large surfaces quickly.

Adding Color and Sparkle

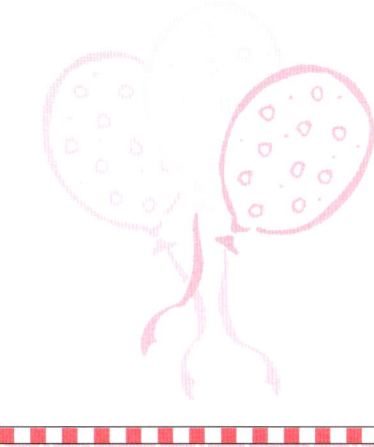

COLORED PENCILS AND MARKERS

When you are using stamps that are primarily outline or "open," you can achieve stunning results by coloring in the image after it is stamped.

Stamp the outline image with a dark ink on any kind of paper if you are going to color with markers. If you are going to use colored pencils, you must stamp on matte or non-glossy paper. (The pencil will not show clearly on glossy paper.) When the ink is dry, color in the image on your paper just as you would in a coloring book. To obtain bright colors, use fine-tip markers, and for a softer, lighter feeling, try colored pencils.

You can achieve subtle gradations of color with colored pencils. The harder you press, the darker the color will appear. (Be careful not to push right through the paper.) You can layer one color over another to create depth, shadows, etc. Colored pencils often look better against a soft outline, which you can create by using the technique outlined earlier: that is, press the stamp on the ink pad or ink the stamp with a marker, tap it once lightly on scrap paper before stamping the image onto your paper. For example, if you are using black ink, this method will give you a gray outline.

WATERCOLOR

There are many ways to give your stamped artwork the look of a watercolor painting. First, choose a stamp that has large open areas that can be filled in with color. Stamp the image using permanent ink, or emboss it to make the ink permanent. Watercolor also works well when you want to paint a shadow alongside an image.

Using watercolor pencils is easy, and when you wet them with water on a brush their colors run like paint.

Experiment with the following methods of using watercolor pencils to add interesting color to your project:

❖ Color in the image with your watercolor pencil, just as you would with markers or

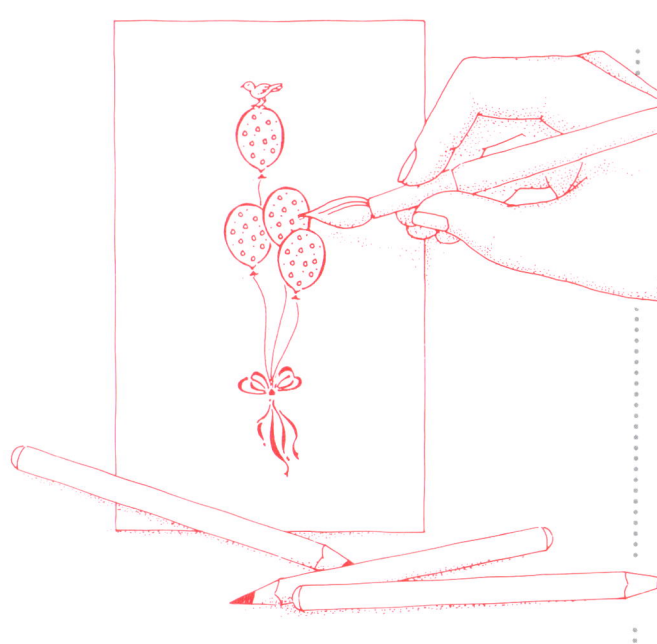

Brush with a small amount of water to blend the colors in the stamped image.

❖ Dip the pencil in water and draw directly on either wet or dry paper to produce the strongest color.

❖ You can also remove pigment from the tip of the pencil, using a moistened brush, and then transfer the pigment to your stamped image, as in traditional watercolor painting. When you want to mix colors, create a palette on a separate piece of paper and blend the colors together with a wet brush. Apply the color to your stamped image.

When you want to achieve a lighter, more transparent look, color your markers onto a piece of aluminum foil or other nonporous surface. Pick up the color from the foil with a wet paintbrush. Paint in your design. You can mix the colors as with any watercolor.

Blenders, designed to blend ink from brush markers, are available with a brush point. They can be used like a wet paintbrush and are convenient when water is not available.

regular colored pencils. Then use a clean, moistened brush or a fine-mist spray bottle to apply a small amount of water, blending the colors as you wish.

❖ To create more intense colors, wet your paper and draw with dry watercolor pencils. Use heavy watercolor paper for this technique. Thin paper may tear easily when wet.

$\mathcal{O}$f course, watercolor paint itself can be used to brighten up your projects. You can use pigment and dye re-inkers, or watercolor paint from a tube as your color source. Lightly moisten your brush (you don't have to use a very expensive brush, but also, don't use a brush that does not have a flexible, finely shaped point when wet) with a small amount of tap water. Brush the slightly moistened paintbrush over the pigment or dye ink. Apply the color directly to your stamped design. Moisten the brush again if the ink starts to dry. Repeat the process with all the other colors until your entire design is complete.

$\mathcal{Y}$ou may find that your paper curls when wet, but it should flatten out again as it dries. If it does not dry flat, place the paper between heavy books overnight. The less water you use (and you shouldn't be using very much), the less problem you will have with curling paper.

CHALKS

$\mathcal{C}$halks create soft, light colors, especially when applied with a little pressure. Chalks are available pressed into squares or sticks, and can be used on almost any kind of paper stock. Apply chalk sticks as you would any crayon or pencil. Chalk squares can be applied with your fingers, cotton swabs, sponges, etc. Spraying your chalk drawings with a fixative, which is available in any rubber-stamp store, makes them permanent.

Stamp three cabbage roses on black glossy paper, emboss them with white embossing powder, and then color the embossed images with chalk. Clean around the outside of the image with a damp sponge.

Glitter

$\mathcal{A}$dd excitement, sophistication, and sparkle to your projects with glitter-filled glue. Apply the glitter glue to accentuate specific areas of your stamped design. Simply tip the container upside down and gently squeeze the bottle as you drag the tip along the line you are decorating, or dab lightly on the spot you wish to highlight. (We have applied glitter to the fireworks card, project number 32.) Allow the glue to dry for 2 to 4 hours. Glitter glue is great for filling in or outlining stamped images, and for adding dimension to your designs.

$\mathcal{I}$f glitter glue is not glittery enough for you, sprinkle additional dry glitter on the image after applying the glitter glue.

$\mathcal{Y}$ou can add glitter of different colors to crystal glitter glue. Gold glitter gives a very rich effect. You can also add glitter and glue separately for more control. Glue is available in pens with many different-sized tips.

$\mathcal{N}$ever put glue directly on the rubber stamp die, since it will ruin the rubber. If your stamp should pick up some glitter, you can remove it by tapping the sticky side of a piece of transparent tape on the rubber die.

$\mathcal{T}$he application of glue should be the last step in the execution of your project.

Adding glitter to the candles is the last step to making this charming card.

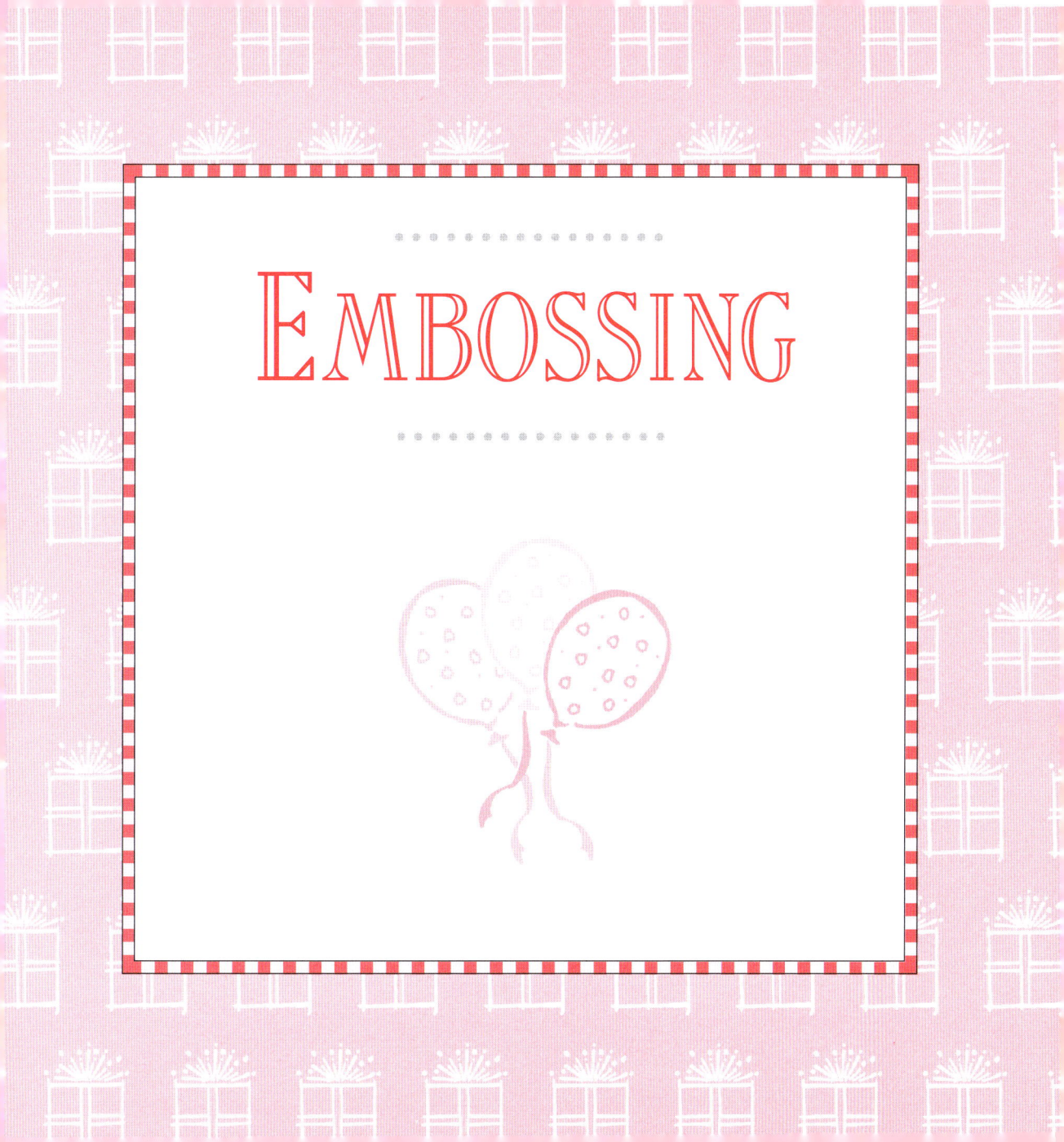

Embossing

Embossing with Ink

*E*mbossing involves heat-treating a stamped print to create a raised, shiny, or metallic impression. It is a stunning, professional-looking technique that you will want to explore as your stamping abilities develop.

*E*mbossing makes a durable impression on all types of paper as well as on other surfaces, such as wood and terracotta. Embossed images are permanent on most surfaces; they do not fade with heat, light, or time.

*P*igment inks are best to use for embossing because of their slow-drying qualities. Embossing fluid, both clear and tinted, is available in a pad or dauber-topped bottle. (Refills are also available.) There are embossing pens available in clear and colors, with fine, calligraphic, and brush tips.

*M*any different types of embossing powders are available, and each produces a different effect. For example, clear embossing powder enhances the color of the ink, producing a raised and shiny surface. Metallic and colored embossing powders will cover the ink, and tinsel powders will add sparkle. Pearl, iridescent, and psychedelic powders may modify the color of the ink used. Texture powders can give your work the look and feel of cement or terracotta. Detail, fine embossing powder—now available—works well for fine, detailed stamps. This embossing powder will not raise the image as high as other embossing powders. It is most readily obtainable in clear, gold, and black. For the opposite effect—greater height and width—an extra-thick embossing powder is available, and is used primarily for double embossing. New types of embossing powders are being introduced to the marketplace regularly.

*I*n order to emboss, you need a heat source of at least 300 degrees Fahrenheit

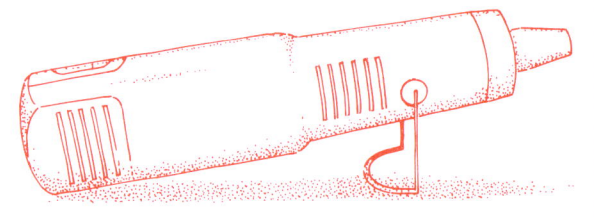

A heat gun—the most efficient tool to use for embossing.

to melt the embossing powder applied to your stamped image. The heat sources most commonly used are a heat gun, a toaster, an iron set on "cotton," an electric stove top, or an oven set at 300 degrees. The commercially available "Craft Heat Gun" is the easiest and most efficient tool because of its steady and even heat flow. It resembles a hand-held hair dryer. Unfortunately, standard hair dryers do not get hot enough to use for embossing.

THE EMBOSSING PROCESS

*A*pply pigment ink, embossing fluid, or ink from a colored brush tip embossing pen to the stamp and stamp the image on the paper. While the ink is still wet, pour embossing powder over the image generously. Make sure your hands are dry and clean because the oil from your hands could transfer to the paper and pick up embossing powder.

*T*ilt the paper and tap off excess powder. The powder will adhere to the stamped image. Use a clean, dry, soft

Sprinkle embossing powder on the stamped image.

Tap off the excess embossing powder.

paintbrush to flick away any powder that sticks to areas other than the image. Cosmetic sponges also work well to remove unwanted powder. If you accidentally brush powder off your stamped image, reapply the powder while the ink is still wet. If you pour several jars of each of your favorite embossing powders into wide-topped plastic food containers you have the option of dipping your cards into the container for faster application. The plastic containers also work well to catch the unused powder.

*H*old the heat gun about 4 to 6 inches from the stamped image to melt the embossing powder. Apply the hot air in a slow circular motion until the entire image is embossed. You will see the powder melt and rise. If you are using any of the alternate sources of heat mentioned above, move the paper in a circular motion, applying the heat to the underside of the paper. Continue heating just long enough for the powder to melt. (Of course, adult supervision is required whenever children are using any of these heat sources.)

Rotate the heat gun in a circular motion while aiming the heat at the shaped image.

THE FOLLOWING TIPS SHOULD HELP YOU BECOME ADEPT AT EMBOSSING:

❖ The color of dark paper may change when heat is applied. The original color will usually return once the paper cools. Be sure to test on a scrap of paper first.

❖ Be careful not to overheat the powder. Overheating may flatten out and dull the embossed image and/or scorch your paper.

❖ To avoid smudges, do not touch the embossed image while it is still hot. Let it cool and harden before touching it.

❖ Use a clothespin or tongs to hold small pieces of paper and to keep your fingers away from the heat source.

❖ If you are embossing several cards at the same time, you can stamp and apply the powder to all the cards before applying the heat source.

❖ If you find that heat warps the paper, let it cool and then flatten it by placing it under a heavy book. Slip a sheet of clean paper between the embossed image and the book, and let it sit for at least an hour.

Special Embossing Techniques

You can use an embossing pen or brush-tip embossing marker to highlight or fill in and emboss areas of a previously stamped image. If the outline of your stamped image was embossed, you can begin this process immediately; if the outline was not embossed, it is best to wait for the ink to dry completely. The embossing powder may stick to the outline as well as the area you have just filled in with the embossing pen or marker if the ink is not completely dry.

An embossing pen can also be used to correct flaws. Draw in areas that did not emboss, and then reapply the powder and heat. You can use glue sticks to emboss stunning borders, hand-drawn designs, or written greetings. The best glue stick to use is one containing liquid glue in a pen form. These pens are available with various writing tips.

Multiple Powders on One Image

To achieve an unusual effect, use various colors of embossing powder on the same image. Start by inking the entire stamp with one shade of pigment ink or embossing fluid. Sprinkle the desired embossing powders, one at a time, on specific sections of the image, tapping off the excess powder before applying the next color. Heat the embossing powder only after all the colors have been applied. This technique works best with metallic powders on solid images. Try using gold, silver, and copper on a leaf or sun stamp for a sensational effect.

EMBOSSING A FRAME OR BORDER

For a thin, uneven border, hold the card upright and pull the edge through pigment ink or embossing fluid. Dip the card into the embossing powder and heat. For a wider border, try using a chiseled-point glue stick or embossing pen. Lay the card stock on your work surface. Using the edge of the card as your guide, run the glue stick along the edge to the desired thickness.

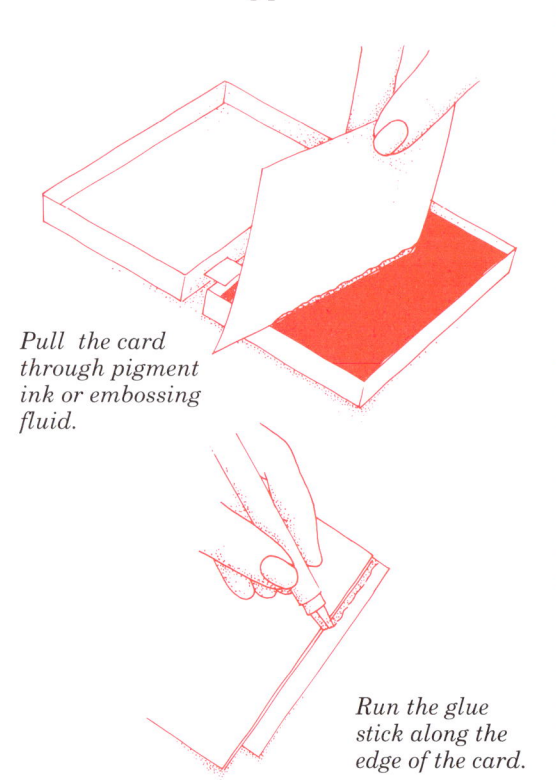

In creating both types of borders, emboss only two edges at a time. This will allow you to hold the card while heating it without transferring the powder to areas you don't want to emboss.

A third method for embossing a frame or border is to place a special lift-off dry adhesive on the area you want to emboss. Be sure that all sections of the adhesive sheet are securely attached to your paper before removing the lift-off paper and applying the embossing powder. Heat as instructed above.

To make a more whimsical frame for a stamped image, use a ballpoint embossing pen to draw a line, dots, or dashes around it, using a ruler or template as a guide. Remember that black ballpoint pens are erasable, so if you make a mistake, it is easily corrected if you use these erasable embossing pens.

Pull the card through pigment ink or embossing fluid.

Run the glue stick along the edge of the card.

Try stamping an image near each corner of your card and using the embossing pen to connect them. This technique is great for framing an address on an envelope, or names on place cards or name tags. Metallic embossing powders work best with this pen. Colored embossing pens are available with various-sized calligraphy and domed tips for writing and drawing.

DOUBLE EMBOSSING

The technique of double embossing works best for a stamped design that will be colored in. Start by embossing the image normally, using the embossing powder of your choice. Color the image using permanent markers or colored pencils. Then, using the clear brush-tip embossing pen or clear embossing fluid on a pad or brush, apply the embossing fluid over the colored image and sprinkle with clear embossing powder. Tap off the excess powder and heat the colored image for a dazzling enameled or stained-glass effect. For even shinier effects, apply additional powder while the image is still hot, and heat it evenly.

You can also use the colored brush-tip embossing markers to fill in the designs and then apply the clear embossing powder and heat to achieve the same results as above.

A clear, ultra-thick embossing powder is available, which works well for the above techniques. In addition, it can be used on card stock to create pins, collage elements, etc.

Moving On

3-D Effects and Shadows

*A*dd dimension to your work for a more realistic or whimsical effect. As you've seen, masking an image and stamping another image "behind" it gives the illusion of depth. This is only one of many techniques to achieve a three-dimensional look.

*W*hen you want an image to literally stand out from the others on the page, stamp it onto your card, then re-ink and stamp the image again on another sheet of card stock. Cut out the image and apply a small piece of double-sided foam tape (available at rubber-stamp and office-supply stores) to the back of the image. For a 3-D effect, position the cut-out image directly over the first image you stamped on the card. Use more layers of tape to achieve various heights in your overall design.

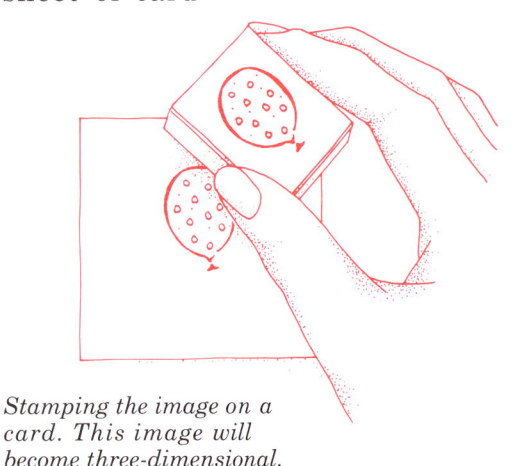

Stamping the image on a card. This image will become three-dimensional.

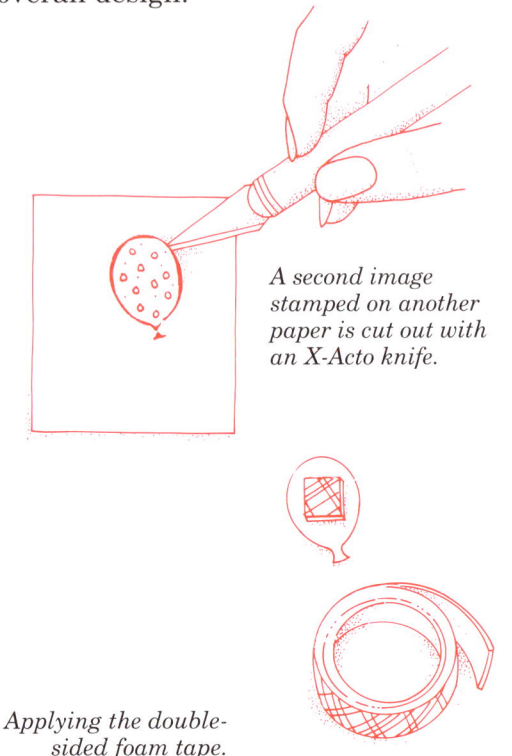

A second image stamped on another paper is cut out with an X-Acto knife.

Applying the double-sided foam tape.

A three-dimensional balloon looks like it is rising off the card.

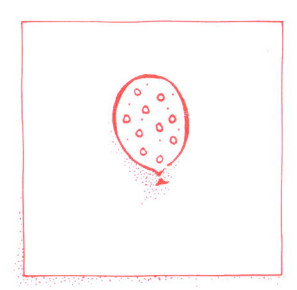

*F*or another three-dimensional look, you can stamp an entire image on a card, and then, using an X-Acto knife, cut out part of it and bend the cut edges forward. This works best with a symmetrical design. Our bow works well, as do the leaves of the flowers and the wings of the dragonfly.

*A*nother way you can create depth in your design is to stamp an image in one color, and then stamp the same image in a second color about 1/16 inch away (usually up and off to one side). Don't forget to clean the stamp between inkings.

*T*he addition of a shadow gives a natural dimension to your artwork. You can create a shadow by drawing a light line along the outside edge of an image with markers. Determine where you want the light to be coming from. The light source should affect each object in your design in the same way. If you imagine the light source in the top right-hand corner of your paper, you would add the shadow below and to the left of each image by drawing a line with a light gray, blue, or even lavender marker along the outer edge.

Adding a shadow to the stamped image creates a natural dimension.

The Illusion of Motion

If you want to make an image appear to be moving, first ink your stamp and stamp it on the paper. Lift the stamp off the paper and, without re-inking it, re-stamp only the "trailing" portion of the design several times, close together and in the direction from which you want the image to appear to be coming.

Another way to show movement is to stamp the image and, without re-inking or lifting the stamp, drag it backwards.

A dragonfly soars across the page.

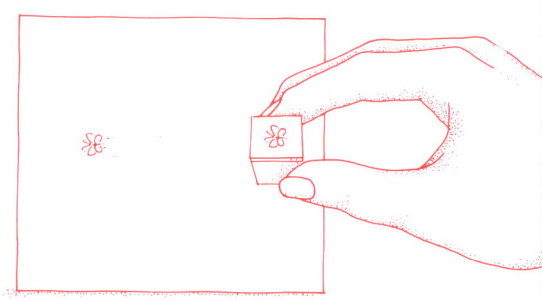

Dragging the image across the page to create visual movement.

Pop-Ups and Pop-Outs

Pop-ups and pop-outs do just that. An image appears to jump out at you as you open the card, or extends beyond a folded edge of the card. Cards made using the following techniques are simple to execute but are guaranteed to surprise and please the recipients.

Select a stamp that will fit within the dimensions of the card you are designing. Stamp the image that will pop up onto a separate card or index stock. Color it as you wish, and then carefully cut it out with a pair of scissors or X-Acto knife. This cut-out image must be attached to a base to allow it to pop up when the card is opened.

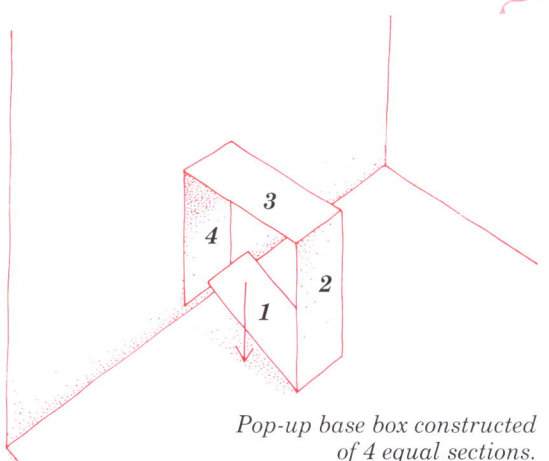

Pop-up base box constructed of 4 equal sections.

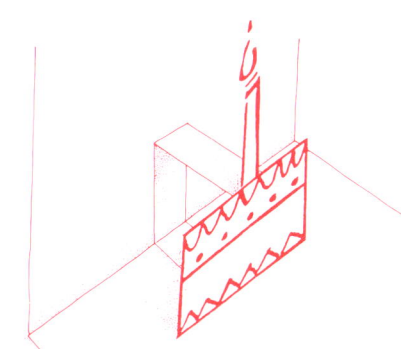

A birthday cake pops up from the center of the fold.

To make a pop-up base, cut out a strip of card stock narrower than the pop-up image. Cut a base strip 4 inches long and 1/2 inch wide. Crease and fold the strip at 1-inch increments. Open your card so that it lies flat, with the inside facing up. Decide at what horizontal point you want to place the pop-up image. Glue section 1 to the bottom of the card at that point, and glue section 4 to the top of the card so that the two ends of the strip meet at the fold of the card. Gently close the card to confirm that the measurements are accurate. Adjust the position as necessary. The cut-out image is then attached to side 2. It lies flat when the card is closed and will automatically pop up when the card is opened.

This is one of the simplest ways to create a pop-up card. As you gain more experience creating pop-up cards you can experiment with different-sized bases.

When selecting pop-up images it is important that the height of the stamped image plus the length of section 1 of the base fits within the height of the card. If the pop-up image is too large it will protrude beyond the edges of the folded card and look haphazard.

There is another simple way to construct a base for the pop-up element from the card itself. With the card closed, measure along the fold, 2 inches from each side. At those two points, draw 1-inch-

A pop-up platform base is created from the card itself.

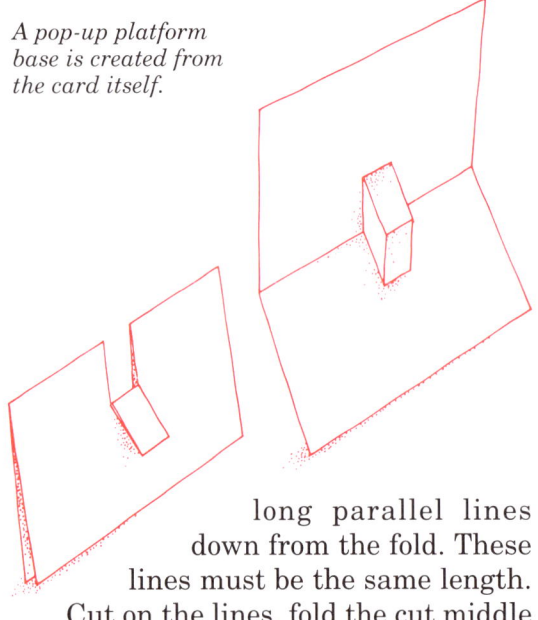

long parallel lines down from the fold. These lines must be the same length. Cut on the lines, fold the cut middle section over the front of the card and press down to crease. Turn the card over, fold the same section in the opposite direction, toward the back of the card. Open the card and press the middle (cut) piece up from behind to form a box shape or platform on which you will place your pop-up image. It is sometimes helpful to work from the front using a pencil to pull the base forward. Close the card. The base will fold forward inside the card. Stamp the inside of the card and attach the image to the pop-up base.

Carefully apply a thin layer of glue around the outside edges of the card. Open a second card and place the cut card inside the uncut card, matching the center folds. Press the two cards together; close the card gently, pulling the pop-up base toward you.

You need not be limited to one platform or base. You can make as many as you wish—a whole town's worth—and even pile one platform on top of another, as long as you always cut on a fold. Remember to experiment with scrap paper first.

You can learn about other methods for creating pop-ups by consulting any one of the many books on the subject that

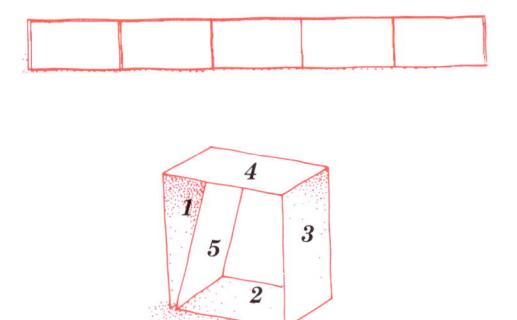

Pop-out base box constructed of 5 equal sections.

are available in the arts-and-crafts sections of most bookstores and libraries.

A pop-out card is similar to a pop-up, but the image can pop out from anywhere on your card. Unlike a pop-up image, a pop-out image does not have to be placed at the fold. Stamp the image that will pop out from the card onto card or index stock (sturdy paper). Color the image and cut it out.

To construct a pop-out card, cut out a base similar to the one for pop-ups, but with 5 equal parts instead of 4. Glue section 1 to section 5 to form a square box. Next, attach the already-glued-together sections 1 and 5 to the card anywhere in your design. Glue your cut-out image to section 3. The pop-out image will lie flat when the card is closed. Once the card is opened, pop out the image by simply lifting it up.

To make a card or place card with an image that pops up above the fold-line, lay the paper or card flat and stamp part of the image, as much as half, above the fold-line. Use an X-Acto knife to cut around the part of the stamped image that is above the line. Score at the fold-line but do not score through the image. Fold the card or place card, and the image will then pop up. See our project number 40.

REVERSING AN IMAGE

*W*hen you want an image on a stamp to face in the opposite direction, use the technique called reversing. Stamp gently onto a flat rubber surface, such as a large eraser, with pigment ink. (Pressing too hard may cause the ink to spread on the rubber.) While the ink is still wet, stamp the eraser onto your artwork using extra pressure. This reverse image will be lighter in color than the initial stamping using the same ink. Therefore,

The portion of the image stamped above the fold-line of a place card is cut out so it will pop up above the standing place card.

if you want to print the original next to the reversed image for a mirrored effect, stamp the reversed image first, and then, without re-inking the stamp press it onto your paper.

Stamp first onto a flat rubber surface using pigment ink.

Stamp using the original stamp on the paper last.

Immediately stamp the rubber surface or eraser onto paper.

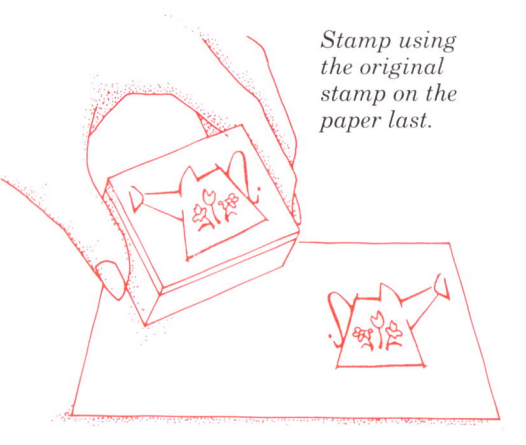

It is important to clean the eraser surface immediately after stamping. Use a damp paper towel and clean the eraser the same way you clean your stamps. Flat, rubber-surfaced stamps designed specifically for reversing an image are available.

FABRIC STAMPING

Rubber stamping on fabric is a great way to personalize clothing, add dazzle to your plain napkins, and make unique gifts. You can stamp on almost any fabric, but those with smooth textures will give you the best results. To stamp on fabrics you can use permanent inks, fabric paints, transfer ink, or embossed pigment ink. All of these methods are described in the following paragraphs.

Both the type of fabric and the method you choose will affect the results. Therefore, always test the stamps and ink on a scrap of your fabric before beginning your project. When you want to color in an outlined image, be sure to use permanent pens designed for use on fabric.

Before you begin, wash the fabric to remove any sizing, but do not use fabric softeners. Iron the fabric to remove wrinkles. You may find it helpful to use an embroidery hoop to support a delicate fabric while stamping. Because the ink may bleed through the fabric, put a piece of poster board under the fabric before you begin. If you are working on a T-shirt, be sure to put the board inside the shirt, between the front and back.

If you are printing on a loosely knit fabric, bond freezer paper onto the wrong side of the garment to hold the fabric firm, to keep it from stretching, and also to prevent the ink from bleeding through to the back of the garment. To bond freezer paper to the fabric, press the paper shiny-side down with an iron set for synthetics. When your project is finished, simply pull off the paper.

When you are working on a knit garment that will be stretched when worn, such as leggings or tights, you may want to stretch the fabric before stamping to avoid having a distorted image. Turn the garment inside out and stretch it to the same degree that it will be stretched when it is worn. To keep the fabric

Stamping on stretchy fabric is most successul when you first stretch and then tape the inside or reverse of the fabric to keep it flat. When the design is complete remove the tape.

Applying fabric paint to a rubber stamp with a small foam brush.

The tulip design stamped on a cloth napkin adds a decorative note.

There are two types of permanent fabric ink. The first dries quickly, and you must use a solvent-based cleaner to remove the ink from your stamps. It is available in a dauber-topped bottle and ink pad. Apply the ink directly to the stamp with the dauber and then stamp onto your fabric. It is possible to apply several colors to one stamp at the same time with this product. Permanent fabric inks are also available in stamp pads that are useful for repetitive stamping of the same color. Because this ink dries quickly, the pad requires re-inking often.

The second type of permanent ink is also available in stamp pads, is slow drying, and can be washed off your stamp with water. The images become permanent once they are heat-set with an iron. This ink can be used on paper when you wish to watercolor the image after stamping. Heat the image to dry the ink before applying the color.

Fabric paints come in a wide range of colors. The easiest way to apply fabric paint to a stamp is to use inexpensive foam brushes or foam pads sold at any rubber-stamp or hobby store. Keep a sup-

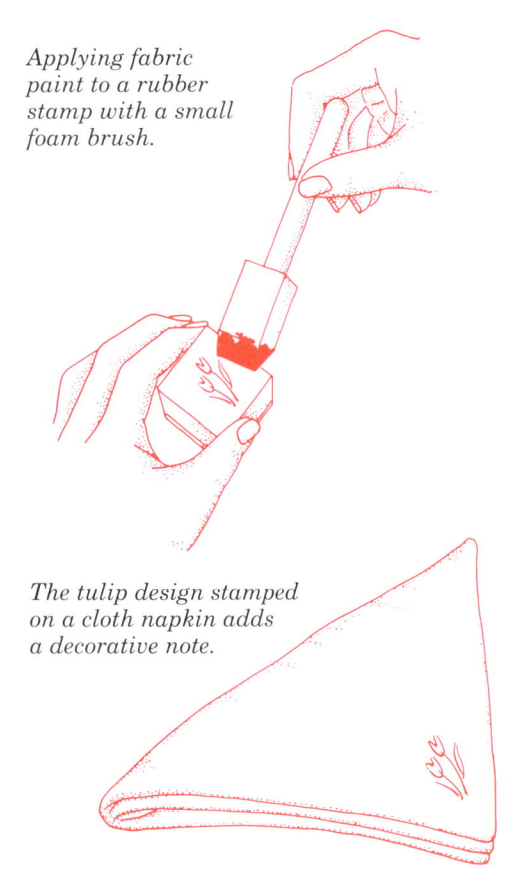

stretched while you are working, attach self-adhesive packing tape where you will be stamping designs. Turn the garment right-side out. After stamping the design, pull the tape off and the fabric will return to its original shape.

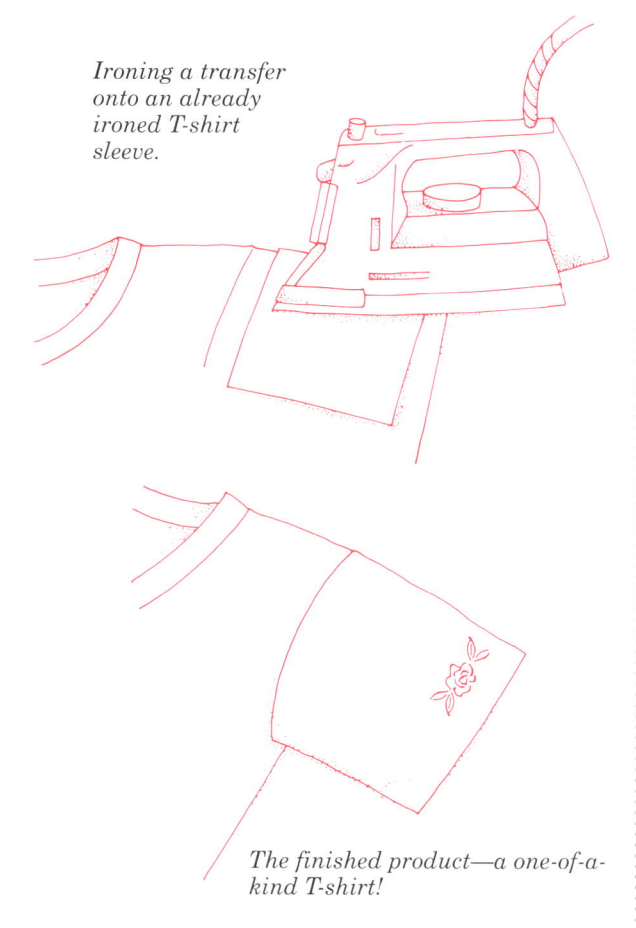

Ironing a transfer onto an already ironed T-shirt sleeve.

The finished product—a one-of-a-kind T-shirt!

ply of cotton swabs handy to clean any area of the stamp that may pick up excess paint before stamping. Because most fabric paints do not become permanent until they dry, you can clean your stamps and brushes with water while the paint is still wet. Some fabric paints require heat-setting to become permanent.

*F*abric paints can be used to paint or sponge directly onto the fabric prior to stamping to create a background. Use masking tape to outline areas you want to keep free of paint.

*T*ransfer ink allows you to stamp a design on paper and then use an iron to transfer the design onto fabric. These inks are available in pads of various colors, and will work well on any paper. When you are satisfied with the images you have stamped on paper, simply iron them on the fabric as directed. Transfer ink works best on fabric that is smooth and contains some polyester. Don't forget that when you use a transfer process you will end up with a mirror image of the original design, so this technique will not work with words.

*Y*ou may want to embellish your stamped designs by using fabric puff-paint and glitter pens designed to be permanent when applied to fabric. Use glue designed for fabric to affix rhinestones and trinkets.

STAMPING ON WOOD AND OTHER SURFACES

*I*nexpensive, unfinished wood products can be purchased in craft stores and decorated with rubber stamps. Before stamping, sand the wood to create a smooth surface. You may also decide to paint or stain the wood before starting. Plan your design while keeping in mind that small images are easier to stamp on curved surfaces.

*U*se permanent ink or acrylic paint, and test your colors on a similar piece of wood, since they produce different shades on various woods. Stamp the design and let the ink dry thoroughly before adding additional color. You can use fabric markers to color in easily, or use the paint on a paintbrush. Embossing on wood will add a metallic or shiny finish to your design. Use the same techniques you used on paper. Be sure to test, because applying heat may cause some undercoat paints to bubble.

*A*ny object that requires washing should be given a protective finish after stamping. We recommend using a spray finish because applying a fixative with a brush may cause the paint to run.

*T*he same process used to stamp on wood also works well on papier-mache boxes. A stamped recipe box with matching stamped recipe cards makes a wonderful gift. You might even add some of your favorite recipes. A stamped picture frame surrounding your favorite little one makes a great gift for Grandma and Grandpa.

*Y*our stamps will work on glass, metal, ceramics, or hard acrylic surfaces if you use permanent ink designed for these finishes. Pigment ink and embossing powder can be used, but the image will not be as durable. Glass stains or paints are available if you wish to add color to your designs.

*C*lay pots can also be decorated with stamps. After wiping the pot to remove any dust, spray the outside with clear acrylic spray and let it dry. Plan your design and use fabric ink or fabric paint to stamp the pot. When the ink is dry, seal it with an acrylic spray. Insert a plastic pot into the clay pot before using it to hold live plants. Clay pots are also fun to use as unique gift baskets, or to hold flowering bulbs like amaryllis or narcissus.

Mounting Stamps

You may decide that you would like to have your stamps mounted onto wood blocks. This is very easy to do, and is something you may enjoy doing yourself. First, you need a cushion between the rubber die and the mount. There are cushions designed specifically for rubber-stamp mounting, but you can also use craft foam, or even foam shoe inserts. For mounts, consider scraps of wood, wooden blocks, plastic boxes, empty thread spools, or empty jars. To begin, firmly pull the rubber die from the foam mounting and trim the die using scissors. Cut close to the design, but be careful not to undercut the image. Use rubber cement to mount the stamp to the cushion. Once the glue has set, cut the cushion to the same size or slightly larger than the die. Then, again using rubber cement, attach the cushion and stamp to your mount. Be sure the die is parallel to the straight edge of the mount.

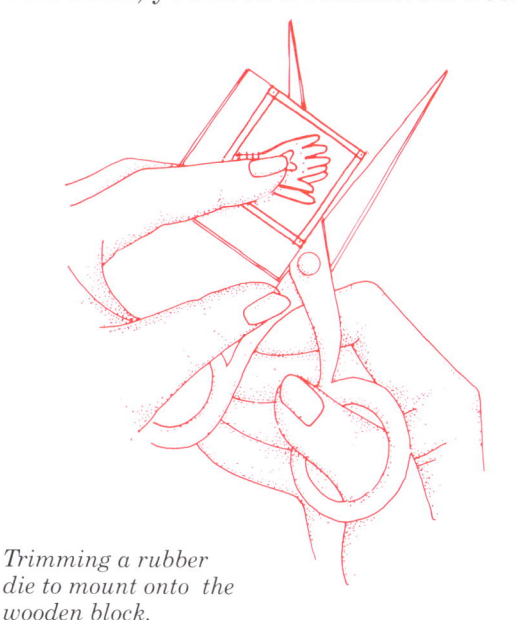

You can print a label or index on the back of a wooden block by stamping the image onto the wood prior to mounting it, using pigment ink or permanent ink. You can also index the stamp by stamping on a piece of paper and attaching it to the block with heavy-duty clear tape. For accuracy in printing, it is important to place the index of your stamp in the same position on the top of your block as the die is on the bottom.

Trimming a rubber die to mount onto the wooden block.

MAKING A STAMP

*T*o create a simple design, such as a star, cut the shape out of self-adhesive foam. It is easy to cut with scissors, and will adhere to a hard surface for stamping. Compressed cellulose sponge, another material used for stamp-making, is also easy to work with.

*D*raw or stamp your design on the sponge and cut it out. Then wet the sponge to expand its thickness. The sponge does not need to be attached to a block for stamping. Craft punches in many shapes and sizes can be used to punch shapes out of the sponge. Both the foam and the sponge can be used with any ink. You can purchase foam specially designed for making stamps at most rubber-stamp and craft stores. We used a compressed cellulose sponge to stamp the squares in project number 31 to form a checkerboard frame.

CARVING A STAMP

*T*o create a stamp with a lot of detail, use carving tools and large flat erasers. Draw directly onto the eraser, keeping in mind that the image you stamp will be the reverse of what you carve.

*A*nother option is to draw onto tracing paper using a soft lead pencil. Blacken the portions of the design that you want to print. Place the design face down on the eraser and rub firmly across the back of the paper with a blunt object to transfer the pencil drawing from the paper to the eraser. This is the easiest way to carve words. Cut away the

Carving a stamp of your own design is very rewarding.

Drawing first on tracing paper and then rubbing that image onto an eraser.

unmarked portions of the eraser. Use tools made for linoleum carving or any other small craft knives to cut the rubber. Make cuts at least 1/8 inch deep.

Tip: For safety, always cut away from yourself.

USING THE COMPUTER

When making greeting cards, thank-you cards, or invitations, the computer can be your best friend. It is much more fun to design and make invitations if you don't need to write the pertinent information each time. Most printers will accept card stock, but if yours does not, print on text-weight paper and copy onto card stock before making your card. We have used the computer to design many of the cards illustrated in this kit.

If you don't have a computer, use a typewriter to type the information, cut and paste the words where you want, and copy onto card stock before stamping the card.

Copiers are readily available for a low cost and are invaluable as you design cards. Copy the illustrations on pages 74-78 and enlarge or reduce them as you wish. In project 41 we enlarged the number 3. In the projects with birdhouses (see the template) we enlarged or reduced them to fit the card we wanted to create. You will want to copy and enlarge the box patterns to fit the gift you are enclosing.

PATTERNS

$\mathcal{U}$se these patterns to create some of the interesting three-dimensional projects we have made. We used this explosion card insert pattern to create project 37. The box patterns were used for projects 47 and 48. You can enlarge or reduce all these patterns as needed on a copier.

TEMPLATES

$\mathcal{Y}$ou can make your own stencils by copying these templates. They are useful for creating instant interesting backgrounds for your stamping projects. You can use the templates to create masks, as on page 35, or trace the outline onto your card. You can vary the size by enlarging or reducing the template on a copier.

NUMERALS

$\mathcal{T}$race and use the numerals on page 104, or use the numeral template included in the kit to create additional greetings or messages for your hand-stamped cards or presents.

TRIANGLE BOX

Enlarge with a copier to the appropriate size.

Box One

Enlarge with a copier to the appropriate size.

Box Two

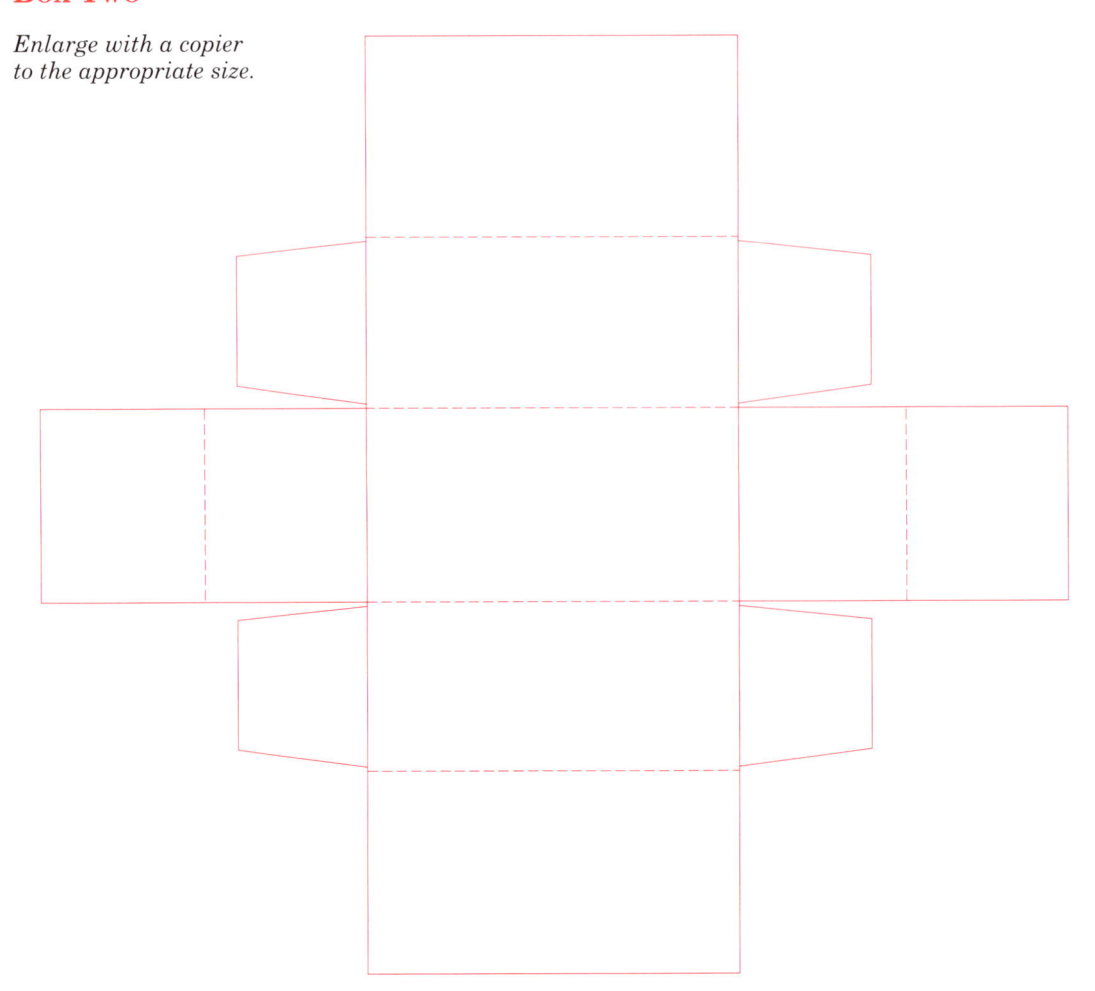

Enlarge with a copier to the appropriate size.

Party Hat

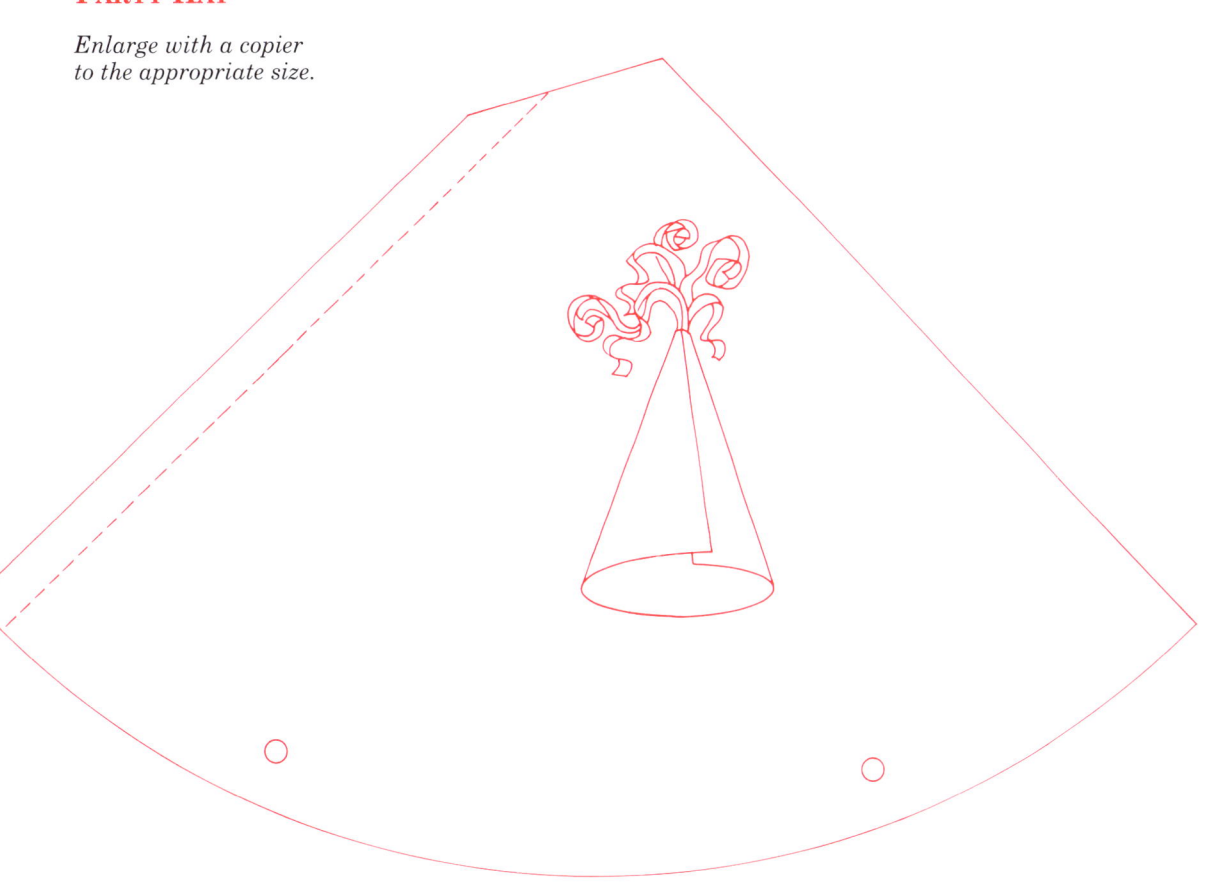

Enlarge with a copier to the appropriate size.

EXPLOSION CARD

❖ *Begin with a square piece of text-weight paper*

❖ *Make valley folds diagonal*

❖ *Turn paper over and mountain fold the center*

❖ *With the mountain fold up, the paper will "collapse" into a triangle shape*

❖ *Fold the ends of the top layer to the center, turn over and repeat on the other side*

❖ *Open up and gently "squash fold" the four corners (push them inward)*

❖ *Attach the folded paper to the inside of a card with glue or double-stick tape*

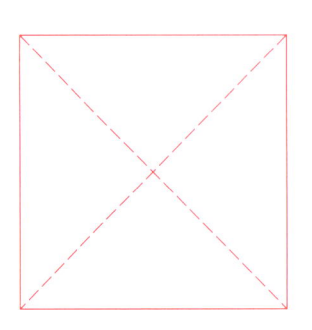

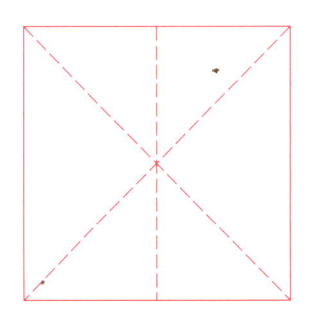

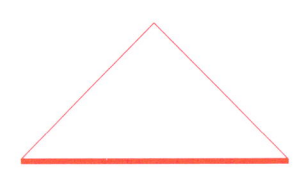

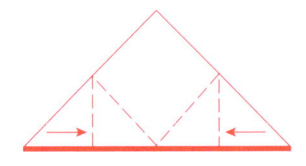

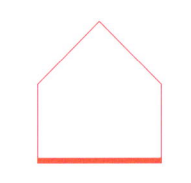

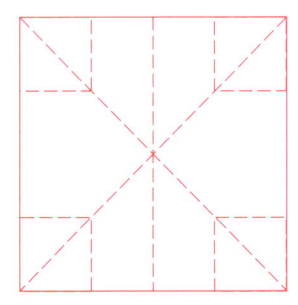

Special Projects

Stamp-A-Birthday™ Special Projects

If you have read this far, you have all the information you need to complete the projects shown in full color on the following pages. Instructions for completing these projects come after the colored pages. These projects have been designed to jump-start your creativity. You may choose to follow the instructions precisely, just like a recipe, and recreate the projects for yourself, or you may prefer to just use them as inspiration, a source book of ideas for your own creations.

Have fun, and don't underestimate your own unique creative ability!

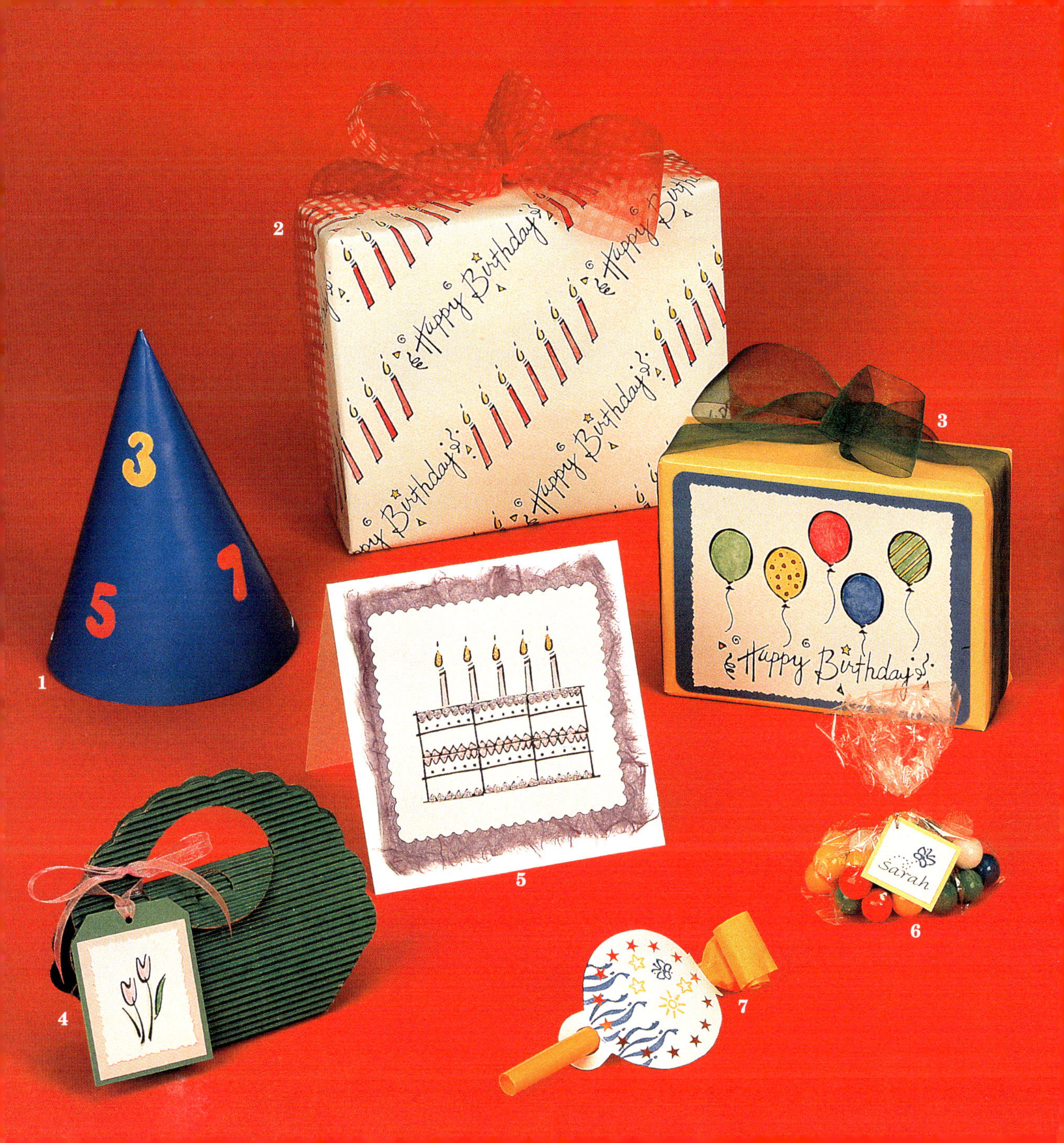

2
3
Happy Birthday
1
5
Sarah
6
4
7

8 9 10 11 12 13

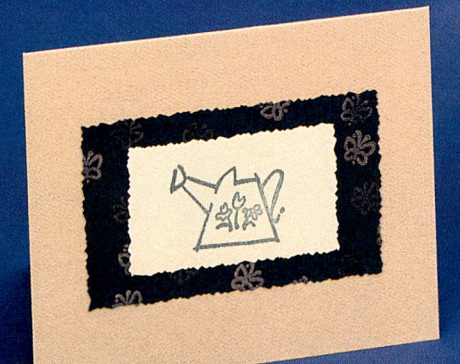

14

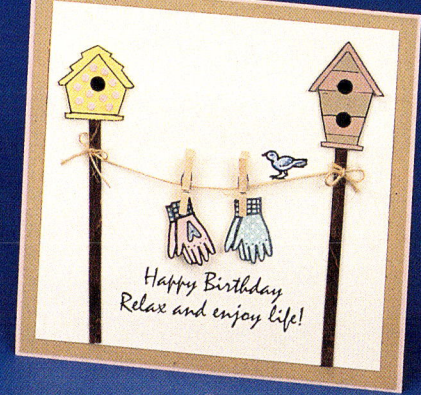

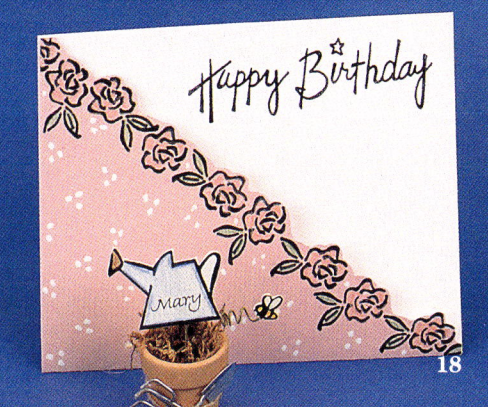

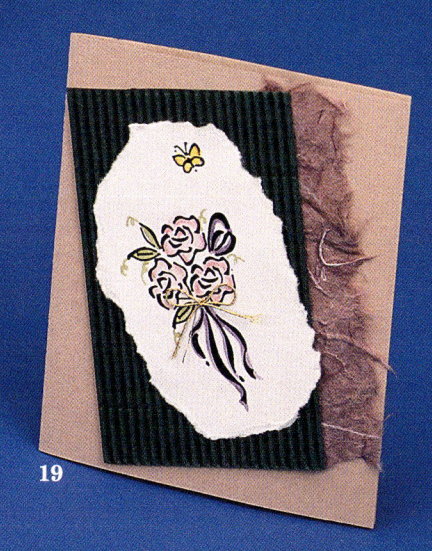

15

16

17

18

19

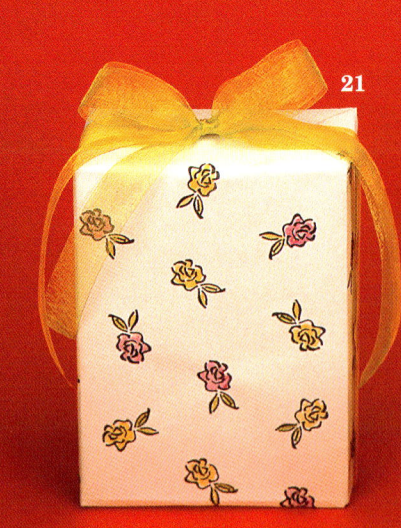

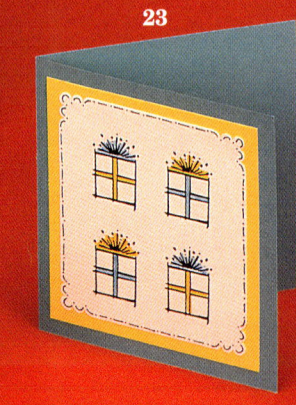

20

21

22

23

24

25

26

27

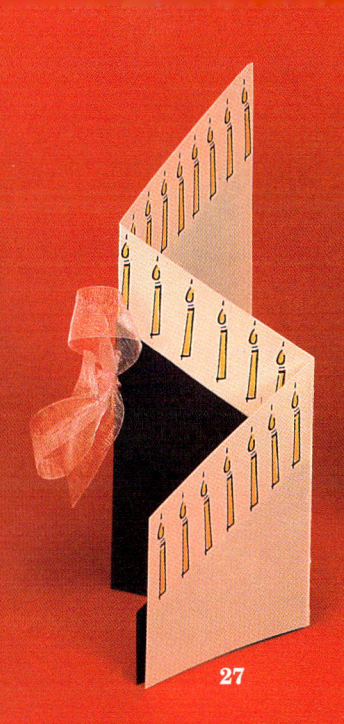

28

29

30

31

32

33

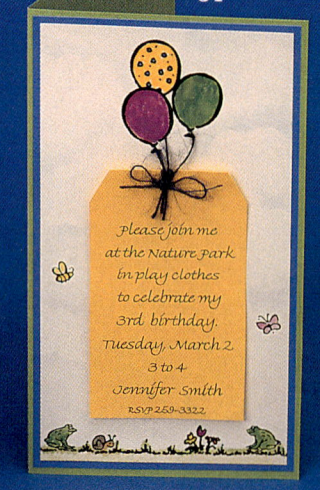

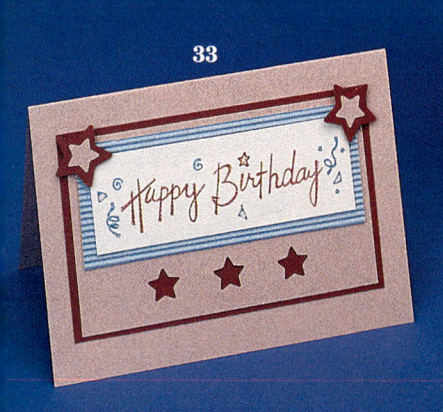

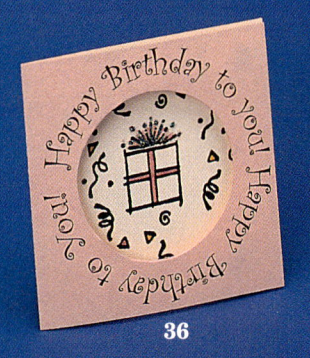

34

35

36

37

38

39

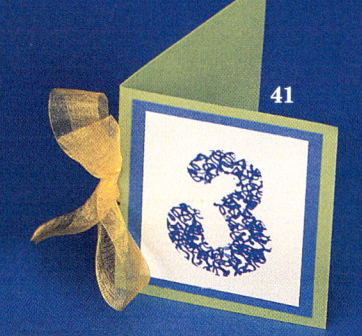

40 Mackenzie

41

42

43

44

45

46

47

48

49

50

Project Number 1

STAMPS: None

SUPPLIES: Paper Party Hat, Colored Paper, Scissors, Pencil, Paper Adhesive

TIPS & TECHNIQUES: Using the sample numbers on page 104, trace or copy them onto colored paper, and glue onto the party hat.

Project Number 2

STAMPS: "Happy Birthday," Candle

SUPPLIES: Black Ink, Colored Pens or Pencils, Gift Wrap

TIPS & TECHNIQUES: Alternate stamping the "Happy Birthday" and a series of candles diagonally across the wrapping or poster paper. Color in the candles, stars, and confetti on the "Happy Birthday." You may want to stamp one candle for each year of age.

Project Number 3

STAMPS: "Happy Birthday," Balloon

SUPPLIES: White Card Stock, Contrasting Card Stock, Colored Gift Wrap, Black Fine Line Pen, Black Brush Marker, Colored Pens or Pencils, Decorative Scissors, Paper Adhesive

TIPS & TECHNIQUES: Wrap gift. Cut white paper approximately one inch smaller than the side of the box. Stamp the "Happy Birthday" in black near the bottom of the paper. Stamp balloons or the outline of the balloon using a black brush marker. Draw stripes on one balloon and color all of them. Draw strings with a fine line pen. Cut the edge of the paper with decorative scissors, back it with a contrasting paper, and apply to the side of the box.

Project Number 4

STAMPS: Tulips

SUPPLIES: White & Green Card Stock, Light Pink Handmade Paper, Colored Pencils or Pens, Party Toy, Decorative Scissors, 1/8-Inch Hole Punch, Ribbon, Paper Adhesive

TIPS & TECHNIQUES: To make the tag, on white card stock that has been cut with decorative scissors, stamp the tulips and color in with pink and green. Attach onto the pink homemade paper and then mount onto the green stock. Punch a 1/8-inch hole in the top of the tag and attach to the party favor with the pink ribbon. We purchased a child's corrugated paper purse as the favor, but any party gift will work just as well.

Project Number 5

STAMPS: Cake, Candle

SUPPLIES: Silver Card, White Card Stock, Decorative Paper, Black Brush Marker,

Colored Pens or Pencils, Decorative Scallop-Edged Scissors, Masking Material, Pink, Purple, & Yellow Liquid Appliqué, Glitter, Paper Adhesive

TIPS & TECHNIQUES: On the white card stock, stamp the cake once, mask the cake, and stamp another next to and above the first one, overlapping it just slightly. Repeat until you have a large cake. Mask the top and stamp the number of candles desired. Color and apply pink and purple liquid appliqué to the frosting on the cake and yellow for the candle flame. Apply glitter and heat to puff. Liquid appliqué is a product that can be found at craft, sewing, and rubber stamp stores. Cut around the edge of the card stock with scallop decorative scissors and glue to the decorative paper before you mount it on the card.

PROJECT NUMBER 6

STAMPS: Butterfly

SUPPLIES: White and Colored Card Stock, Colored Brush Markers, Fine Line Pen, 1/8-Inch Hole Punch, Gold Cord, Ribbon

TIPS & TECHNIQUES: We used a computer to type the names on card stock. Cut a square tag with the name on the bottom edge. Apply ink to the butterfly and stamp above the name. Draw dots from the name to indicate the butterfly's flight pattern.

PROJECT NUMBER 7

STAMPS: Heavenly Bodies, Butterfly, Streamers

SUPPLIES: Blue & Yellow Brush Markers, Party Toy, White Card Stock, Star Punch, Craft Knife, Scissors

TIPS & TECHNIQUES: Draw a circle with a 2 1/2-inch diameter on the card stock. Add a tab, with a hole in the center, to the top and bottom. The hole should be large enough to slip over the party favor. Decorate the circle with the stamps and punch star-shaped holes around the outside of the circle.

PROJECT NUMBER 8

STAMPS: Watering Can, Framed Garden Gloves, Garden Tool

SUPPLIES: Postage Stamps of Garden or Flower Designs, Gold Embossing Powder, Pigment Ink, Embossing Supplies, Brush Markers, Colored Card Stock, Paper Corrugator, Paper Adhesive

TIPS & TECHNIQUES: Find papers that coordinate with your postage stamps and glue each one on a paper that is approximately 1/4 inch larger than the stamp. Tear small scraps of the same paper and stamp the gloves from the garden glove frame on one and emboss the garden tool on the other. Arrange the five items in a pleasing manner on paper that you have corrugated with a paper corrugator, which is available at stamp or craft stores. Emboss the watering can in gold on the paper. Mount the corrugated paper on a slightly larger dark card.

Project Number 9

STAMPS: Dragonfly

SUPPLIES: Black & Green Ink, Three Shades of Green Card Stock, Ivory Card Stock, Decorative Scissors, Paper Adhesive, Colored Pens or Pencils

TIPS & TECHNIQUES: Stamp green dragonflies in an allover pattern on the back piece of light green card stock. Stamp black dragonflies on three pieces of ivory card stock, color, and cut square with the decorative scissors. Mount each one onto two pieces of card stock to frame. Lastly, arrange all three vertically on the background paper and mount on the ivory card.

Project Number 10

STAMPS: Tulips, Sprig

SUPPLIES: Green Brush Marker, Colored Pens or Pencils, Ivory, Yellow, & Two Shades of Pink Card Stock, Green Corrugated Paper, Heart Punch, Decorative Scissors, Glue

TIPS & TECHNIQUES: Cut a piece of green corrugated paper in the shape of a flower box. In green stamp several tulips on the ivory card stock. Ink one tulip at a time and stamp to fill in the flower box. Stamp the sprig in green all across the base of the flowers. Color in the tulips. Glue the flower box in place and glue a punched-out hot pink heart to the front. Trim the ivory card stock with decorative scissors. Mount on a slightly larger yellow piece of card stock and finally on a pink card.

Project Number 11

STAMPS: Gift, "Happy Birthday"

SUPPLIES: Ivory Card Stock, Black Brush Marker, Colored Pens or Pencils, Craft Knife

TIPS & TECHNIQUES: Ink the bottom only of the gift and repeatedly ink and stamp it on the card to form an oblong frame. Stamp them right next to each other but do not overlap. With a craft knife, cut out an oblong opening in the center and stamp "Happy Birthday" on the inside so it shows through to the front. We did not ink the confetti on the sides of the "Happy Birthday" stamp. Color in the frame to form a checkerboard.

Project Number 12

STAMPS: Watering Can, Butterfly

SUPPLIES: Ivory, Teal, & Peach Card Stock, Colored Brush Markers, Pigment Ink, Decorative Scissors, Paper Adhesive

TIPS & TECHNIQUES: On a small piece of ivory card stock, stamp the watering can in dark green. On the dark teal card stock stamp the butterfly in an overall design using pigment ink (dye ink will not show on dark paper). Cut both pieces of paper with the decorative scissors and mount on the peach card.

PROJECT NUMBER 13

STAMPS: Flower, Bird

SUPPLIES: Tan Corrugated Paper, Two Shades of Green & Two Shades of Tan Card Stock, Scrap of Black Paper, Green & Brown Brush Markers, Brown or Black Fine Line Pen, Colored Pencils, 1/4-Inch Hole Punch, Birdhouse Stencil, Foam Mounting Tape, Paper Adhesive

TIPS & TECHNIQUES: On the light tan card stock, draw lines to form branches with a fine line brown or black pen. Stamp the leaves of the flower stamp several times on the branches using a green brush marker. Mount this paper onto the tan corrugated paper. Mount the corrugated paper onto the light green card stock leaving a larger border at the bottom. Stamp the bird on the bottom border. Mount everything on a green card. Use the template to make the birdhouse. Cut out and color. Punch out a hole in black paper and use what was punched out to form the opening for the bird. Mount it on the branch with foam mounting tape. Color the bird.

PROJECT NUMBER 14

STAMPS: Butterfly

SUPPLIES: Light Tan, Gold, & Brown Card Stock, Decorative Scissors, Commemorative Postage Stamps, Brown Fine Line Pen, Brown Brush Marker, Paper Adhesive

TIPS & TECHNIQUES: Find a commemorative postage stamp of a butterfly and select colors of paper to complement the stamp. Mount the postage stamp on a piece of paper to frame it. Cut this piece of paper out with decorative scissors. For the background paper stamp the butterfly in brown to form an overall design. Mount this on the card leaving a larger border at the bottom. In this space write the word "Happy" in dashes that then lead up to a stamped butterfly. The word "Happy" should appear as his flight pattern.

PROJECT NUMBER 15

STAMPS: Bird, Framed Garden Gloves

SUPPLIES: Two Coffee Stirrers, Tiny Clothespins, Tan Cord, Ivory, Tan, Pink, Yellow, & Black Card Stock, Tiny Polka Dot–Printed Paper, Brown & Black Brush Markers, Colored Pencils, 1/8-Inch Hole Punch, 1/4-Inch Hole Punch, Foam Mounting Tape, Paper Adhesive

TIPS & TECHNIQUES: We used a computer to

type the greeting on the card stock. You could also use a typewriter, press-on letters, or write the message. Color the coffee stirrers with the brown brush markers, tie a piece of tan cord between them to form a clothesline, and glue the poles to the card. Stamp the bird so he appears to be sitting on the line and color. Stamp the gloves on the pink paper. For the second set of gloves, ink everything except the heart and stamp on printed paper, color, and cut out. Hang one from each clothespin. Use the template to create the birdhouses on yellow and tan card stock. Draw stripes on the tall tan one and color. Punch out 1/8-inch circles from pink paper and glue the dots on the yellow house. Out of black card stock, punch out three 1/4-inch circles and glue on for doors. Mount the birdhouses on top of the poles with foam mounting tape. Mount on tan paper to frame and then put on a pink card.

PROJECT NUMBER 16

STAMPS: Balloon, "Happy Birthday"

SUPPLIES: White & Teal Card Stock, Pink Checked Paper, Star Corner Rounder, Black Brush Marker, Black Fine Line Pen, Colored Pens or Pencils, Paper Adhesive

TIPS & TECHNIQUES: On white card stock stamp in black, one balloon and two balloon frames. Draw, with the black fine line pen, the flag and tails on the balloons. With the black brush marker, ink the "Happy" of "Happy Birthday" and stamp it twice inside the flag. Stamp the star from the same stamp around the words. Color the balloons and with a light blue marker draw a shadow on two sides of the flag to give it dimension. Use a star corner rounder punch to round the corners and put a star in each corner. Layer onto pink printed paper and then onto teal card stock to frame. Mount on a white card.

PROJECT NUMBER 17

STAMPS: Bee, Watering Can

SUPPLIES: Miniature Flowerpot & Garden Tools, Tan Cord, Green Floral Wire, Dried Plant Moss, Ivory Card Stock, Plaster of Paris, Colored Pens or Pencils, Paper Adhesive

TIPS & TECHNIQUES: To construct this placecard, tie the tiny garden tool to the front of the clay pot with the tan cord. Type or write the name on card stock. Ink only the outline of the watering can and stamp it over the name. Color and cut out. Stamp the bee on card stock, color, and cut out. Tape pieces of floral wire to the back of both the bee and watering can and glue to the card stock. Cut them out again. Wrap the wire from the bee around a narrow pencil to coil. Mix a small amount of plaster of paris according to the manufacturer's directions and put in the pot to hold the wires firm. Fill with dried moss to cover the plaster.

Project Number 18

Stamps: Flower, "Happy Birthday"

Supplies: Pink & White Card Stock, Black Brush Marker, White Pen, Colored Pens or Pencils, Paper Adhesive

Tips & Techniques: Cut a piece of pink card stock for the card. In black, stamp the flower stamp diagonally across the card changing the direction of the flower and sometimes inking only the flower without the leaf. Cut along the line of flowers. Cut a piece of white card stock and glue to the inside of the card. Ink only the words on the "Happy Birthday" and stamp on the inside so it shows above the row of flowers. Color the flowers and with the white pen draw three dots in a group, randomly across the front of the card.

Project Number 19

Stamps: Flowers, Bow, Streamers, Butterfly

Supplies: White & Lavender Card Stock, Dark Green Corrugated Paper, Handmade Decorative Paper, Black Brush Marker, Colored Pens & Pencils, Gold Cord, Paper Adhesive

Tips & Techniques: Ink only the flower part of the flower stamp and stamp it three times to form a bouquet. Stamp two leaves at the top and one at the bottom, between the flowers. Add one side of the bow between the flowers and place the streamers at the bottom. Stamp the butterfly above the bouquet. Form a palette by putting some ink from pink, purple, yellow, and green pens on a piece of plastic or aluminum foil. Using a wet brush, pick up each color from the palette and paint the stamped design. Tear the paper around the arrangement, add a gold string bow, and assemble the collage and mount on the card.

Project Number 20

Stamps: Snail, Bee, Butterfly, Dragonfly, Bird

Supplies:: Black Ink, Colored Pens or Pencils, Tan Corrugated Paper, Handmade Paper, Marbled Paper, Ivory & Rust Card Stock, Paper Adhesive, Photo Corners

Tips & Techniques: Stamp, in black, the dragonfly on ivory card stock and cut into a square. Stamp three snails vertically on a piece of ivory card stock the same height as the dragonfly; stamp the butterfly on a piece the same width as the snails. Cut the butterfly square. Stamp the bee and bird on two pieces the same heights as the butterfly. Together they should not be as wide as the dragonfly. Color and assemble them on top of a square of tan corrugated paper. Feather the edges of handmade paper with water, pulling out the fibers of the papers. Place the handmade paper on top of a square of rust card stock. The corrugated paper will be glued on top of the handmade paper. Using photo corners, attach everything to the card of marbled paper mounted on top of the rust card stock.

PROJECT NUMBER 21

STAMPS: Flower

SUPPLIES: White Gift Wrap or Poster Paper, Black Brush Markers, Colored Pens or Pencils, Ribbon

TIPS & TECHNIQUES: Randomly stamp the flower all over the paper using black ink. Color the flowers and wrap the gift.

PROJECT NUMBER 22

STAMPS: Tulips, Flowerpot

SUPPLIES: Navy & White Card Stock, Decorative Paper, Calendar, Black Brush Marker, Colored Pens or Pencils, Masking Material, Paper Adhesive

TIPS & TECHNIQUES: To construct the base, take a piece of navy card stock 9 x 5 inches and fold in half. Score 1 1/2 inches in from both ends and fold in on the score lines. When glued together this will make the bottom. On the backside, score a line 1/2 inch in from the first score line. This will make a pleat that allows the calendar to lean back. On white card stock, stamp the flowerpot in black. Mask the pot and stamp the tulips, one at a time, to fill the pot. Color and tear around the edge. Mount on marbled paper and attach to the base with the calendar.

PROJECT NUMBER 23

STAMPS: Gift

SUPPLIES: White, Lime, & Turquoise Card Stock, Black Brush Marker, Scallop Corner Punch, Colored Pens, Black Fine Line Pens, Paper Adhesive

TIPS & TECHNIQUES: Stamp the gift, in black, four times on the white card stock. Color in the ribbon and bow on the gifts. Cut the paper into a square and punch out each corner. Draw dots and dashes in black, around the outside edge. Attach to the lime card stock and finally onto the turquoise card.

PROJECT NUMBER 24

STAMPS: Cake, Candle

SUPPLIES: Gift box, White & Green Card Stock, Decorative Scissors, 1/16-Inch Hole Punch, Black Fine Line Pen, Black Brush Marker, Colored Pens or Pencils, Masking Material, Ribbon, Paper Adhesive

TIPS & TECHNIQUES: Purchase a ready-made gift box, (or construct one out of navy card stock). On white card stock, stamp the cake, mask, and stamp the candles on the cake. Color and cut out with scallop decorative scissors. With a black fine tip pen, draw a dot in the center of each scallop. Attach to a piece of green card stock and tie onto the box.

Project Number 25

STAMPS: Framed Garden Gloves

SUPPLIES: Small Colored Bag, White & Green Card Stock, Black Brush Marker, Ribbon, 1/16-Inch Hole Punch, Colored Pens and Pencils, Paper Adhesive

TIPS & TECHNIQUES: Using black ink, stamp the framed garden gloves on white card stock. Color the gloves and outside frame and cut along the outside of the frame. Attach to the green card stock. Punch a hole in the corner with the 1/16-inch punch and attach to your ribbon with fine cord.

Project Number 26

STAMPS: Dragonfly

SUPPLIES: Satin Ribbon, Gold Embossing Powder, Pigment or Embossing Ink, Embossing Supplies

TIPS & TECHNIQUES: Using pigment or embossing ink, stamp the dragonfly along the ribbon. Emboss using the gold powder. We suggest embossing three dragonflies at a time to insure the ink stays wet enough to hold the powder. Remember to have a dry paintbrush or cosmetic sponge handy to whisk away unwanted particles of embossing powder before you apply heat.

Project Number 27

STAMPS: Candle

SUPPLIES: Lightweight Vellum Paper, Navy Blue Card Stock, Pigment or Embossing Ink, Embossing Supplies, Colored Pens, 1/8-Inch Hole Punch, Organdy Ribbon

TIPS & TECHNIQUES: Draw a light pencil line, to be erased later, diagonally across the vellum paper starting on the right side 3 inches up from the bottom and going to the upper corner on the left side. Cut along the line and fold the paper in thirds. Working on one section at a time, stamp the candles, using pigment or embossing ink, in a row with the pencil line as your guide. Emboss the candles in gold. On the first and last sections they will be on the front of the paper, and on the middle section they will be stamped on the back of the paper. Color in the candles and flame. Fold a piece of navy card stock into thirds and cut it diagonally to fit under the candles. Punch two holes in the back fold and tie the two papers together with a piece of ribbon.

Project Number 28

STAMPS: Streamers, Grass, Heart, Sprig

SUPPLIES: Ivory, Tan, & Navy Blue Card

Stock, Colored Brush Markers, Sponge, Paper Adhesive

TIPS & TECHNIQUES: Cut a flowerpot shape out of tan card stock. Ink the grass stamp in brown or dark tan and stamp it upside down on the flowerpot to indicate the shadow under the rim of the pot. Mark the location of your pot on the card stock so you know where to place flowers but do not glue. The flowers are made using the streamer stamp. Ink with brush markers and stamp in a circle with the top of the streamer being the center of the flowers. To give the flower dimension, stamp some without re-inking. This will result in a lighter impression. Draw in green stems. Stamp the outline of the heart stamp in green to make leaves. Sponge green to fill in the leaf and draw a line in the center of some. Lightly stamp the sprig in as floral filler. You will want to remove most of the green ink on your scrap paper first before stamping the filler. Attach the flowerpot and assemble the card with glue.

PROJECT NUMBER 29

STAMPS: Sprig, "Happy Birthday"

SUPPLIES: Red, White, Black, & Blue Card Stock, Green & Blue Brush Markers, Colored Pens, Star-Shape Punch, 1/4-Inch Hole Punch, Tan Cord, Foam Mounting Tape, Paper Adhesive

TIPS & TECHNIQUES: Repeatedly stamp the sprig to resemble branches on a tree. You will want to vary the direction you stamp and the part of the sprig you fill in with ink. It will also look more realistic if you use several different shades of green ink. On a separate piece of white card stock draw the birdhouses using the template, and decorate. We used the star from the "Happy Birthday" stamp on one of them, and a star punched out of red on another. Punch out four black circles with the hole punch and attach to the birdhouses for openings. Attach the houses to the card with foam mounting tape. Glue the bows on top of each house. Assemble the card.

PROJECT NUMBER 30

STAMPS: Heavenly Bodies

SUPPLIES: Black Ink, Red & Yellow Pens, Ruler, Gift Wrap or Poster Paper

TIPS & TECHNIQUES: Draw a grid on your paper using a ruler and a red pen. Ink one at a time the star, moon, and sun and stamp each in a square stamping the same design diagonally across the paper. Repeat until the paper is full. Wrap your gift.

Project Number 31

Stamps: "Happy Birthday," Framed Garden Gloves

Supplies: Ivory, Green, & Navy Blue Card Stock, Blue & Green Brush Markers, Compressed Cellulose Sponge, Paper Adhesive

Tips & Techniques: Using a blue brush marker, ink the words "Happy Birthday," but do not ink the confetti on either side. Stamp it in the middle of the ivory card stock. Cut a piece of compressed cellulose sponge 1/2 inch square. Wet the sponge and using blue ink, stamp it in a checkerboard design around the words. Using a green brush marker, ink the heart found in the center of the framed garden gloves and stamp it in each open square. Assemble the card using a paper adhesive.

Project Number 32

Stamps: Gift

Supplies: Red, White, & Blue Card Stock, Red & Blue Brush Markers, Fine Line Black Pen, Glitter, Fine Line Glue Pen, Paper Adhesive

Tips & Techniques: Type, using a computer or a typewriter, or write across the bottom of a piece of white card stock "Happy Birthday America." Apply red and blue ink to the bow section of the gift and stamp it up and down to form fireworks. Add glue with a fine line glue pen and add glitter. Assemble the card.

Project Number 33

Stamps: "Happy Birthday"

Supplies: Light Blue & Light & Dark Burgundy Card Stock, Turquoise Corrugated Paper, Large & Small Star Punches, Burgundy & Blue Brush Markers, Foam Mounting Tape, Glitter, Paper Adhesive

Tips & Techniques: Use two colors of ink on the "Happy Birthday" stamp. Apply burgundy ink on the words and blue on the confetti and stamp on the light blue paper. Cut out and mount on turquoise corrugated paper. Layer onto the top of the light burgundy stock and punch three small hearts in the bottom frame. Finish layering the card. Punch two large stars from the dark burgundy stock and two from the light burgundy and glue them together. Mount them above the "Happy Birthday" with foam mounting tape.

Project Number 34

Stamps: Frogs, Balloon, Bee, Butterfly, Snail, Watering Can, Grass

Supplies: Green, Blue, Ivory, & Yellow

Card Stock, Black Ink, Colored Pens or Pencils, String, Sponge, Cloud Stencil, 1/4-Inch Hole Punch, Craft Knife, Masking Material, Paper Adhesive

TIPS & TECHNIQUES: Type, using a computer or a typewriter, or write your invitation on yellow card stock and cut into a tag shape. Punch a 1/4-inch hole in the top. Use this tag as your guide when planning the size of the card. Stamp the grass stamp near the bottom of the ivory card stock. Ink one frog at a time and stamp them one on each side. Be sure to wash the stamp well and dry it before stamping the second image. Ink only the flowers on the watering can, stamp, and color them. Ink, stamp, and color the snail, butterfly, and bee. Now, stamp the outlines of the two balloons closest to the top of the tag. Mask the one on the right and stamp the entire balloon over the mask. Use the cloud template and sponge in light blue to create the sky. Use a craft knife to make a tiny slit at the neck of the two bottom balloons and the lower edge of the balloon on the left. Put three pieces of string through the slits and tape to the back. Use the three pieces of string on the front to tie the tag to the card. Complete by gluing the layers to the card.

PROJECT NUMBER 35

STAMPS: "Happy Birthday," Framed Garden Gloves

SUPPLIES: Yellow, Pink, & Turquoise Card Stock, Pink Corrugated Paper, Black Ink, Colored Pens or Pencils, Masking Material, Paper Adhesive

TIPS & TECHNIQUES: Ink only the frame of the framed garden gloves and stamp it on the lower right side of the card. Mask the frame and repeat across the card. Using the numbers found on page 104 draw one in each square. Highlight the box representing the age of the recipient by cutting the number out of pink and the background out of turquoise paper. Stamp "Happy Birthday" in black on a piece of turquoise paper, color in the open areas, and mount onto pink corrugated paper. Glue the corrugated paper on the top of the card.

PROJECT NUMBER 36

STAMPS: Gift, "Happy Birthday"

SUPPLIES: Pink & Ivory Card Stock, Black Ink, Colored Pens or Pencils, Glitter, Craft Knife, Paper Adhesive

TIPS & TECHNIQUES: Type, using a computer or a typewriter, or write "Happy Birthday To You" in a circle on pink card stock. Cut out the center of the circle with a craft knife.

Insert a piece of ivory card stock inside the card and glue down. Stamp the gift in the center, so it shows through the open circle. Ink the confetti on the "Happy Birthday" stamp and stamp it all around the gift. Color the open areas and apply glue and glitter to the bow of the gift.

Project Number 37

STAMPS: "Happy Birthday," Tulips, Butterfly, Sprig, Grass

SUPPLIES: Yellow Card Stock, White Text-Weight Paper, Pink, Green, Burgundy, & Yellow Brush Markers, Paper Adhesive

TIPS & TECHNIQUES: Cut a piece of white text-weight paper into a 5-inch square. Following the pattern and directions on page 78 fold the paper. Ink the "Happy Birthday" stamp in burgundy, the confetti and star in yellow, and stamp on the top half. Stamp the grass, in green, along the bottom. Ink the top of the tulips in pink and the stem and leaves in green using brush markers and stamp them above the grass. Fill in with green sprigs. Stamp yellow butterflies between "Happy Birthday" and the tulips. Cut a 3 x 5 1/2-inch piece of yellow card stock and fold in half for the cover. Refold the stamped paper when the ink is dry and insert into the cover, gluing one side at a time.

Project Number 38

STAMPS: Bow

SUPPLIES: Ivory Card Stock, Pink Handmade Paper, Burgundy Brush Marker, Burgundy Fine Line Pen, Charm, Gold Cord, Craft Knife, Paper Adhesive

TIPS & TECHNIQUES: Type, using a computer or a typewriter, or write the name on the ivory card stock. Cut into a rectangle shape and stamp the bow in burgundy. Use a craft knife to cut a small slit under the bow. String the charm on the gold cord and put both ends through the slit under the bow. Tape to the back. Mount the handmade paper on the card and finally place the rectangle piece on top of the handmade paper.

Project Number 39

Stamps: Frog, Watering Can, Grass

Supplies: Small White Bag, Pink Ribbon, Ivory, Yellow, & Pink Card Stock, Colored Pens or Pencils, Black Brush Marker, Black Fine Line Pen, Decorative Scissors, Rectangle Punch, Paper Adhesive

TIPS & TECHNIQUES: On a square piece of ivory card stock stamp the grass along the bottom. Stamp one of the frogs and the flowers in the center of the watering can on the grass. Draw a word bubble for the frog and print in the message. Cut along the edge with the decorative scissors. Fold the bag, punch two holes in the top, and insert ribbon to close. Layer pink and yellow card stock behind the ivory card and glue everything on the front of the bag.

PROJECT NUMBER 40

STAMPS: Gift

SUPPLIES: Ivory & Purple Card Stock, Black Ink, Colored Pens or Pencils, Purple Fine Line Pen, Craft Knife, Paper Adhesive

TIPS & TECHNIQUES: Cut a piece of ivory card stock the size of a placecard. Lightly mark the center. Stamp the gift, partially over the center of the card. Score on the center line of the card, but do not score over the stamped image. With your craft knife, cut from the score line up and over the design and back to the score line. When you fold the card, the gift will appear to pop up. Draw two parallel lines with a fine line pen near the bottom of the card. Fold a contrasting card and glue under the ivory card.

PROJECT NUMBER 41

STAMPS: "Happy Birthday"

SUPPLIES: Green, Blue, & Ivory Card Stock, Blue Brush Marker, 1/8-Inch Hole Punch, Craft Knife, Ribbon, Paper Adhesive

TIPS & TECHNIQUES: Enlarge the number from page 104 and cut out the number with a craft knife. Place the paper with the number cut out, over the ivory card stock. This is a mortise mask. Ink the confetti on the "Happy Birthday" stamp with blue ink and repeatedly stamp over the mask until the open area is almost completely covered. Layer the ivory paper onto the blue and the blue onto the green card. Punch two holes on the fold of the card and insert a ribbon.

PROJECT NUMBERS 42 & 43

STAMPS: "Happy Birthday," Bow, Balloon, Cake, Candle, Heavenly Bodies

SUPPLIES: Photo Album, Birthday Photos, Purple, Orange, & Gold Acid Free Paper, Printed Background Paper, Black Ink, Orange, Purple, & Gold Brush Markers, Paper Adhesive

TIPS & TECHNIQUES: What better way to use *Stamp-A-Birthday*™ than to remember your birthday forever by creating a memory album. Assemble your photos and determine a color scheme to complement the pictures. In this case we picked up the color of the birthday balloons to use for the papers surrounding the pictures. You want to enhance your photos with color and design, being careful not to overpower them. Using the same background paper and repeating colors and designs all help to tie the pictures together. On project 42 we made a gift with a number 2 by drawing a square topped with the bow stamp. On project 43 each balloon or balloon frame was stamped and cut out of colored paper. The balloon bouquet is constructed by gluing one balloon on top of another. The confetti on both pages comes from the "Happy Birthday" stamp.

Project Number 44

STAMPS: Flower, Framed Garden Gloves, Dragonfly

SUPPLIES: Green Card Stock, Black Brush Marker, Colored Pencils, 1/8-Inch Hole Punch, Ribbon

TIPS & TECHNIQUES: Ink only the frame of the framed garden gloves and stamp it on the card three times. Stamp the dragonfly in the center frame, and the flower in the two end frames. Color with a colored pencil. Punch two holes in the top of the card and add a complementary ribbon.

Project Number 45

STAMPS: Watering Can, Garden Tool, Framed Garden Gloves

SUPPLIES: Calculator Paper, Black Brush Marker, Colored Pencils

TIPS & TECHNIQUES: Cut a length of calculator paper that will wrap around the gift. Alternate images along the paper and color the images. Wrap the gift.

Project Number 46

STAMPS: "Happy Birthday," Framed Garden Gloves

SUPPLIES: White Card Stock, Black Brush Marker, Colored Pens or Pencils, Charm, Ribbon, 1/16-Inch Hole Punch, Craft Knife

TIPS & TECHNIQUES: Ink only the "Happy Birthday," not the confetti, and stamp it just below the center of the card. Stamp the framed garden gloves above the "Happy Birthday." Cut out the center of the frame. Punch two holes on the back of the card, just below the top of the frame, and pull a ribbon through to the front. This will be used to tie on the charm. Color in the frame and the star in "Happy Birthday."

Project Number 47

STAMPS: Tulips, Flowerpot, Snail

SUPPLIES: Pink Card Stock, Coordinating Ribbon, Colored Pencils, Masking Material, Glitter, Paper Adhesive

TIPS & TECHNIQUES: Trace the box on page 74 onto pink card stock. Fold to create the box. Open to stamp the flowerpot near the bottom. Mask the pot and stamp the tulips one at a time in the pot. Stamp the snail alongside the flowerpot. Color in the images and apply glue and glitter along the base of the flowerpot.

Project Number 48

STAMPS: Acorn/Leaves

SUPPLIES: Green Card Stock, Black Ink, Colored Pencils, Fine Line Gold Pen, Ribbon, Paper Adhesive

TIPS & TECHNIQUES: Trace the box pattern on page 76 onto green card stock. Fold to create the box. Stamp the leaves and acorn on each side. Using a colored pencil color in the leaves and top of the acorn. We used a fine line gold pen to outline the leaves and color the bottom of the acorn.

Project Number 49

STAMPS: Heart, "Happy Birthday"

SUPPLIES: Ivory & Navy Blue Card Stock, Black Brush Marker, Colored Pens or Pencils, Curly Gold Wire, Fancy Corner Punch, Scissors, Craft Knife, Paper Adhesive

TIPS & TECHNIQUES: With the black brush marker, ink the words and star on the "Happy Birthday" stamp. Stamp it in the center of a piece of ivory card stock and color the star. Stamp the heart on both sides, one slightly above the words and one slightly below, and color. With the craft knife make a hole in each star inside the heart. Pull three short pieces of curly gold wire through each hole and tape to the back. Use a fancy corner punch on each corner. Cut the navy blue card stock 3/8 inch larger, and using a scissors cut 1/8-inch slits around the card. Stretch the curly gold wire and wrap around the blue card taping the beginning and the end in place on the back. Glue the layers to complete the card.

Project Number 50

STAMPS: Tulip, Bee, Grass

SUPPLIES: White Bag or White Paper, Shirt Board or Cardboard, 1/8-Inch Hole Punch, Black Ink, Colored Pens or Pencils, Black Fine Line Pen, Ribbon, Paper Adhesive

TIPS & TECHNIQUES: To make a gift bag fold over approximately one inch on the long side of a sheet of typing paper. With the fold at the top edge of a book or small box, wrap the paper around it and glue to close. We tried to keep the seam at the side so we could stamp on both the front and back of the bag. Close and glue the bottom as you do when you wrap a gift. For added strength, we cut a piece of cardboard to fit on the bottom of the bag. Gently pleat the sides to complete. Cut a piece of shirt board or light cardboard to fit inside while you stamp. This allows you to stamp without the folds showing. Stamp three tulips and the grass on the bottom and color. Stamp a bee above the tulips. With a black fine line pen, draw dashes to indicate his flight pattern through the flowers. Remove the cardboard, punch two holes in the top, and close with a ribbon.

NUMERALS

CLOUD STENCIL